# On Marriage and
# Concupiscence

# On Marriage and Concupiscence

## St. Augustine

# On Marriage and Concupiscence

Written by: St. Augustine (Nov.13 354 – Aug.28 430)
Translated by Peter Holmes and Robert Ernest Wallis
Revised by: Professor Benjamin B. Warfield, D.D
Updated into Modern U.S English by A.M. Overett (b. 1960)

Published by
Lighthouse Christian Publishing
SAN 257-4330
5531 Dufferin Drive
Savage, Minnesota, 55378
United States of America

www.lighthousechristianpublishing.com

EXTRACT FROM AUGUSTIN'S
"RETRACTATIONS,"
Book II. Chap. 53,
ON THE FOLLOWING TREATISE, "DE NUPTIIS ET
CONCUPISCENTIA."

"I Addressed two books to the Illustrious Count Valerius, upon hearing that the Pelagians had brought sundry vague charges upon us—how, for instance, we condemned marriage by maintaining Original Sin. These books are entitled, On Marriage and Concupiscence. We maintain that marriage is good; and that it must not be supposed that the concupiscence of the flesh, or "the law in our members which wars against the law of mind," is a fault of marriage. Conjugal chastity makes a good use of the evil of concupiscence in the procreation of children. My first treatise contained two books. The first of them found its way into the hands of Julianus the Pelagian, who wrote four books in opposition to it. Out of these, somebody extracted sundry passages, and sent them to Count Valerius; he handed them to us, and after I had received them I wrote a second book in answer to these extracts. The first book of this work of mine opens with these words: "Our new heretics, most beloved son Valerius," while the second begins thus: "Amid the cares of your duty as a soldier."

## ADVERTISEMENT TO THE READER ON THE FOLLOWING TREATISE.

On revising these two Books, which he addressed to the Count Valerius, Augustin placed them immediately after his reply to the discourse of the Arians, which was affixed to the Proceedings with Emeritus. Now these proceedings are stated to have taken place on the 20th of September, in the year of our Lord 418. There can be no doubt, then, that these subjoined books—or, at any rate, the former of them—were written either at the close of the year 418, or in the beginning of the year 419. For, concerning this first book, Augustin says himself: "This book of mine, however, which he [Julianus] says he answered in four books, I wrote after the condemnation of Pelagius and Cœlestius. This," he adds, "I have deemed it right to mention, because he declares that my words had been used by the enemies of the truth to bring it into odium. Let no one, therefore, suppose that it was owing to this book of mine that condemnation had been passed on the new heretics who are enemies of the grace of Christ." From these words one may see at once that this first book was published about the same time as the condemnation of the Pelagians in the year 418.

Soon after its publication it began to be assailed by the Pelagians, who observed that its perusal was producing in the minds of the Catholics much odium against their heresy. One of them, Julianus, influenced with a warm desire of furthering the heretical movement, attacked the first book of Augustin's treatise in four books of his own. Out of these, sundry extracts were culled by some interested person, and forwarded to Count Valerius. Valerius dispatched them from Ravenna to Rome, to

Alypius, in order that he, on returning to Africa, might hand them to Augustin for the purpose of an early refutation, together with a letter in which Valerius thanked Augustin for the previous work which he also mentioned. Augustin saw at once that these extracts had been taken out of the work of Julianus; and, although he preferred reserving his answer to the selections till he had received the entire work from which they were culled, he still thought that he was bound to avoid all delay in satisfying the Count Valerius. Without loss of time, therefore, he drew up in answer his second book, with the same title as before, On Marriage and Concupiscence, which, as we think, must be assigned to the year 420, since the holy doctor wrote it immediately after the expression of thanks for the first book; for it is clearly improbable that Valerius should have waited two years or more to make the acknowledgment of his gratitude.

Moreover, the Valerius whom Augustin dignifies with the title of Illustrious as well as Count, was much employed in public life—not, to be sure, in the forum, but in the field; and from this circumstance we find it difficult to accede to the opinion that supposes him to have been the same person with the Valerius who was Count of the Private Estate in the year 425, Consul in 432, and lastly Master of the Offices under Theodosius the younger in the year 434. These appointments, indeed, had no connection with military service, nor had the prefects of Theodosius anything in common with those of Honorius.

# A LETTER ADDRESSED TO THE COUNT VALERIUS, ON AUGUSTIN'S FORWARDING TO HIM WHAT HE CALLS HIS FIRST BOOK "ON MARRIAGE AND CONCUPISCENCE."

To the illustrious and deservedly eminent Lord and his most dearly beloved son in the love of Christ, Valerius, Augustin sends greeting in the Lord.

1. While I was chafing at the long disappointment of receiving no acknowledgments from your Highness of the many letters which I had written to you, I all at once received three letters from your Grace, —one by the hand of my fellow bishop Vindemialis, which was not meant for me only, and two, soon afterwards, through my brother presbyter Firmus. This holy man, who is bound to me, as you may have ascertained from his own lips, by the ties of a most intimate love, had much conversation with me about your excellence, and gave me undoubted proofs of his complete knowledge of your character "in the bowels of Christ;" by these means he had sight, not only of the letters of which the fore-mentioned bishop and he himself had been the bearers, but also of those which we expressed our disappointment at not having received. Now his information respecting you was all the more pleasant to us, inasmuch as he gave me to understand, what it was out of your power to do, that you would not, even at my earnest request for an answer, become the extoller of your own praises, contrary to the permission of Holy Scripture. But I ought myself to hesitate to write to you in this strain, lest I should incur the suspicion of

flattering you, my illustrious and deservedly eminent lord and dearly beloved son in the love of Christ.

2. Now, as to your praises in Christ, or rather Christ's praises in you, see what delight and joy it was to me to hear of them from him, who could neither deceive me because of his fidelity to me, nor be ignorant of them because of his friendship with you. But other testimony, which though inferior in amount and certainty has still reached my ear from divers quarters, assures me how sound and catholic is your faith; how devout your hope of the future; how great your love to God and the brethren; how humble your mind amid the highest honors, as you do not trust in uncertain riches, but in the living God, and art rich in good works; how your house is a rest and comfort of the saints, and a terror to evildoers; how great is your care that no man lay snares for Christ's members (either among His old enemies or those of more recent days), although he use Christ's name as a cloak for his wiles; and at the same time, though you give no quarter to the error of these enemies, how provident you are to secure their salvation. This and the like, we frequently hear, as I have already said, even from others; but now we have, by means of the above-mentioned brother, received a fuller and more trustworthy knowledge.

3. Touching, however, the subject of conjugal purity, that we might be able to bestow our commendation and love upon you for it, could we possibly listen to the information of anyone but some bosom friend of your own, who had no mere superficial acquaintance with you, but knew your innermost life? Concerning, therefore, this excellent gift of God to you, I am delighted to converse with you with more frankness and at greater length. I am quite sure that I shall not prove burdensome to you, even

if I send you a prolix treatise, the perusal of which will only ensure a longer converse between us. For this have I discovered, that amidst your manifold and weighty cares you pursue your reading with ease and pleasure; and that you take great delight in any little performances of ours, even if they are addressed to other persons, whenever they have chanced to fall into your hands. Whatever, therefore, is addressed to yourself, in which I can speak to you as it were personally, you will deign both to notice with greater attention, and to receive with a higher pleasure. From the perusal, then, of this letter, turn to the book which I send with it. It will in its very commencement, in a more convenient manner, intimate to your Reverence the reason, both why it has been written, and why it has been submitted specially to your consideration.

ON MARRIAGE AND CONCUPISCENCE,

In Two Books,

Addressed to the Count Valerius BY AURELIUS AUGUSTIN, BISHOP OF HIPPO;

written in419 AND 420.

---

Book I.

Wherein He expounds the peculiar and natural blessings of marriage. He shows that among these blessings must not be reckoned fleshly concupiscence; insomuch as this is wholly evil, such as does not proceed from the very nature of marriage, but is an accident thereof arising from original sin. This evil, notwithstanding, is rightly employed by marriage for the procreation of children. But, as the result of this concupiscence, it comes to pass that, even from the lawful marriage of the children of God, men are not born children of God, but of the world, and are bound with the chain of sin, although their parents have been liberated therefrom by grace; and are led captive by the devil, if they be not in like manner rescued by the self-same grace of Christ. He explains how it is that concupiscence remains in the baptized in act though not in guilt. He teaches, that by the sanctity of baptism, not merely this original guilt, but all other sins of men whatever, are taken away. He lastly quotes the authority of Ambrose to show that the evil of concupiscence must be distinguished from the good of marriage.

Chapter 1. —Concerning the Argument of This Treatise.

Our new heretics, my dearest son Valerius, who maintain that infants born in the flesh have no need of that medicine of Christ whereby sins are healed, are constantly affirming, in their excessive hatred of us, that we condemn marriage and that divine procedure by which God creates human beings by means of men and women, inasmuch as we assert that they who are born of such a union contract that original sin of which the apostle says, "By one man sin entered into the world, and death by sin; and so death passed upon all men, for in him all sinned;" and because we do not deny, that of whatever kind of parents they are born, they are still under the devil's dominion, unless they be born again in Christ, and by His grace be removed from the power of darkness and translated into His kingdom, who willed not to be born from the same union of the two sexes. Because, then, we affirm this doctrine, which is contained in the oldest and unvarying rule of the catholic faith, these propounders of the novel and perverse dogma, who assert that there is no sin in infants to be washed away in the laver of regeneration, in their unbelief or ignorance calumniate us, as if we condemned marriage, and as if we asserted to be the devil's work what is God's own work—the human being which is born of marriage. Nor do they reflect that the good of marriage is no more impeachable because the original evil which is derived therefrom, than the evil of adultery and fornication is excusable because the natural good which is born of them. For as sin is the work of the devil, from whencesoever contracted by infants; so man is the work of God, from whencesoever born. Our purpose, therefore, in this book, so far as the Lord vouchsafes us in

His help, is to distinguish between the evil of carnal concupiscence from which man who is born therefrom contracts original sin, and the good of marriage. For there would have been none of this shame-producing concupiscence, which is impudently praised by impudent men, if man had not previously sinned; while as to marriage, it would still have existed even if no man had sinned, since the procreation of children in the body that belonged to that life would have been affected without that malady which in "the body of this death" cannot be separated from the process of procreation.

Chapter 2. [II.]—Why This Treatise Was Addressed to Valerius.

Now there are three very special reasons, which I will briefly indicate, why I wished to write to you particularly on this subject. One is, because by the gift of Christ you are a strict observer of conjugal chastity. Another is, because by your great care and diligence you have effectually withstood those profane novelties which we are resisting in our present discussion. The third is, because of my learning that something which they had committed to writing had found its way into your hands; and although in your robust faith you could despise such an attempt, it is still a good thing for us also to know how to bring aid to our faith by defending it. For the Apostle Peter instructs us to be "ready always to give an answer to everyone that asks us a reason of the faith and hope that is in us;" and the Apostle Paul says, "Let your speech be always with grace, seasoned with salt, that ye may know how ye ought to answer every man." These are the motives which chiefly impel me to hold such converse with you in this volume, as the Lord shall enable me. I have never liked, indeed, to intrude the perusal of any of my humble labors on any eminent person, who is like yourself conspicuous to all from the elevation of his office, without his own request, —especially when he is not blessed with the enjoyment of a dignified retirement, but is still occupied in the public duties of a soldier's profession; this has always seemed to me to savor more impertinence than of respectful esteem. If, then, I have incurred censure of this kind, while acting on the reasons which I have now mentioned, I crave the favor of your forgiveness, and kindly regard to the following arguments.

Chapter 3 [III.]—Conjugal Chastity the Gift of God.

That chastity in the married state is God's gift, is shown by the most blessed Paul, when, speaking on this very subject, he says: "But I would that all men were even as I myself: but every man hath his proper gift of God, one after this manner, and another after that." Observe, he tells us that this gift is from God; and although he classes it below that continence in which he would have all men to be like himself, he still describes it as a gift of God. Whence we understand that, when these precepts are given to us in order that we should do them, nothing else is stated than that there ought to be within us our own will also for receiving and having them. When, therefore, these are shown to be gifts of God, it is meant that they must be sought from Him if they are not already possessed; and if they are possessed, thanks must be given to Him for the possession; moreover, that our own wills have but small avail for seeking, obtaining, and holding fast these gifts, unless they be assisted by God's grace.

Chapter 4. —A Difficulty as Regards the Chastity of Unbelievers. None But a Believer is Truly a Chaste Man.

What, then, have we to say when conjugal chastity is discovered even in some unbelievers? Must it be said that they sin, in that they make a bad use of a gift of God, in not restoring it to the worship of Him from whom they received it? Or must these endowments, perchance, be not regarded as gifts of God at all, when they are not believers who exercise them; according to the apostle's sentiment, when he says, "Whatsoever is not of faith is sin?" But who would dare to say that a gift of God is sin? For the soul and the body, and all the natural endowments which are implanted in the soul and the body, even in the persons of sinful men, are still gifts of God; for it is God who made them, and not they themselves. When it is said, "Whatsoever is not of faith is sin," only those things are meant which men themselves do. When men, therefore, do without faith those things which seem to appertain to conjugal chastity, they do them either to please men, whether themselves or others, or to avoid incurring such troubles as are incidental to human nature in those things which they corruptly desire, or to pay service to devils. Sins are not really resigned, but some sins are overpowered by other sins. God forbid, then, that a man be truly called chaste who observes connubial fidelity to his wife from any other motive than devotion to the true God.

Chapter 5 [IV.]—The Natural Good of Marriage. All Society Naturally Repudiates a Fraudulent Companion. What is True Conjugal Purity? No True Virginity and Chastity Except in Devotion to True Faith.

The union, then, of male and female for the purpose of procreation is the natural good of marriage. But he makes a bad use of this good who uses it bestially, so that his intention is on the gratification of lust, instead of the desire of offspring. Nevertheless, in sundry animals unendowed with reason, as, for instance, in most birds, there is both preserved a certain kind of confederation of pairs, and a social combination of skill in nest-building; and their mutual division of the periods for cherishing their eggs and their alternation in the labor of feeding their young, give them the appearance of so acting, when they mate, as to be intent rather on securing the continuance of their kind than on gratifying lust. Of these two, the one is the likeness of man in a brute; the other, the likeness of the brute in man. With respect, however, to what I ascribed to the nature of marriage, that the male and the female are united together as associates for procreation, and consequently do not defraud each other (forasmuch as every associated state has a natural abhorrence of a fraudulent companion), although even men without faith possess this palpable blessing of nature, yet, since they use it not in faith, they only turn it to evil and sin. In like manner, therefore, the marriage of believers converts to the use of righteousness that carnal concupiscence by which "the flesh lusted against the Spirit." For they entertain the firm purpose of generating offspring to be regenerated—that the children who are born of them as "children of the world" may be born again and become "sons of God." Wherefore all parents who do not beget children with this intention, this will, this purpose, of transferring them from being members of the first man into being members of Christ, but boast as unbelieving parents over unbelieving children, —however circumspect they be in their cohabitation, studiously limiting it to the begetting of children, —really have no conjugal chastity in themselves. For since chastity is a virtue, hating unchastity as its contrary vice, and as all the virtues (even those whose operation is by means of the body) have their seat in the soul, how can the body be in any true sense said to be chaste, when the soul itself is committing fornication against the true God? Now such fornication the holy psalmist censures when he says: "For, lo, they that are far from Thee shall perish: Thou hast destroyed all them that go a whoring from Thee." There is, then, no true chastity, whether conjugal, or vidual, or virginal, except that which devotes itself to true faith. For though consecrated virginity is rightly preferred to marriage, yet what Christian in his sober mind would not prefer catholic Christian women who have been even more than once married, to not only vestals, but also to heretical virgins? So great is the avail of faith, of which the apostle says, "Whatsoever is not of faith is sin;" and of which it is written in the Epistle to the Hebrews, "Without faith it is impossible to please God."

Chapter 6 [V.]—The Censuring of Lust is Not a Condemnation of Marriage; Whence Comes Shame in the Human Body. Adam and Eve Were Not Created Blind; Meaning of Their "Eyes Being Opened."

Now, this being the real state of the question, they undoubtedly err who suppose that, when fleshly lust is censured, marriage is condemned; as if the malady of concupiscence was the outcome of marriage and not of sin. Were not those first spouses, whose nuptials God blessed with the words, "Be fruitful and multiply," naked, and yet not ashamed? Why, then, did shame arise out of their members after sin, except because an indecent motion arose from them, which, if men had not sinned, would certainly never have existed in marriage? Or was it, forsooth, as some hold (who give little heed to what they read), that human beings were, like dogs, at first created blind; and—absurder still—obtained sight, not as dogs do, by growing, but by sinning? Far be it from us to entertain such an opinion. But they gather that opinion of theirs from reading: "She took of the fruit thereof, and did eat; and gave also unto her husband with her, and he did eat: and the eyes of them both were opened, and they knew that they were naked." This accounts for the opinion of unintelligent persons, that the eyes of the first man and woman were previously closed, because Holy Scripture testifies that they were then opened. Well, then, were Hagar's eyes, the handmaid of Sarah, previously shut, when, with her thirsty and sobbing child, she opened her eyes and saw the well? Or did those two disciples, after the Lord's resurrection, walk in the way with Him with their eyes shut, since the evangelist says of them that "in the breaking of bread their eyes were opened, and they knew Him"? What, therefore, is written concerning the first man and woman, that "the eyes of them both were opened," we ought to understand as that they gave attention to perceiving and recognizing the new state which had befallen their body. Now that their eyes were opened, their body appeared to them naked, and they knew it. If this were not the meaning, how, when the beast of the field and the fowls of the air were brought unto him, could Adam have given them names if his eyes were shut? He could not have done this without distinguishing them; and he could not distinguish them without seeing them. How, too, could the woman herself have been beheld so clearly by him when he said, "This is now bone of my bone, and flesh of my flesh"? If, indeed, any one shall be so determined on caviling as to insist that Adam might have acquired a discernment of these objects, not by sight but by touch, what explanation will he have to give of the passage wherein we are told how the woman "saw that the tree," from which she was about to pluck the forbidden fruit, "was pleasant for the eyes to behold"? No; "they were both naked, and were not ashamed," not because they had no eyesight, but because they perceived no reason to be ashamed in their members, which had all along been seen by them. For it is not said: They were both naked, and knew it not; but "they were not ashamed." Because, indeed, nothing had previously happened which was not lawful, so nothing had ensued which could cause them shame.

Chapter 7 [VI.]—Man's Disobedience Justly Requited in the Rebellion of His Own Flesh; The Blush of Shame for the Disobedient Members of the Body.

When the first man transgressed the law of God, he began to have another law in his members which was repugnant to the law of his mind, and he felt the evil of his own disobedience when he experienced in the disobedience of his flesh a most righteous retribution recoiling on himself. Such, then, was "the opening of his eyes" which the serpent had promised him in his temptation—the knowledge, in fact, of something which he had better been ignorant of. Then, indeed, did man perceive within himself what he had done; then did he distinguish evil from good, —not by avoiding it, but by enduring it. For it certainly was not just that obedience should be rendered by his servant, that is, his body, to him, who had not obeyed his own Lord. Well, then, how significant is the fact that the eyes, and lips, and tongue, and hands, and feet, and the bending of back, and neck, and sides, are all placed within our power—to be applied to such operations as are suitable to them, when we have a body free from impediments and in a sound state of health; but when it must come to man's great function of the procreation of children the members which were expressly created for this purpose will not obey the direction of the will, but lust has to be waited for to set these members in motion, as if it had legal right over them, and sometimes it refuses to act when the mind wills, while often it acts against its will! Must not this bring the blush of shame over the freedom of the human will, that by its contempt of God, its own Commander, it has lost all proper command for itself over its own members? Now, wherein could be found a more fitting demonstration of the just depravation of human nature because of its disobedience, than in the disobedience of those parts whence nature herself derives subsistence by succession? For it is by an especial propriety that those parts of the body are designated as natural. This, then, was the reason why the first human pair, on experiencing in the flesh that motion which was indecent because disobedient, and on feeling the shame of their nakedness, covered these offending members with fig-leaves; in order that, at the very least, by the will of the ashamed offenders, a veil might be thrown over that which was put into motion without the will of those who wished it: and since shame arose from what indecently pleased, decency might be attained by concealment.

Chapter 8 [VII.]—The Evil of Lust Does Not Take Away the Good of Marriage.

Forasmuch, then, as the good of marriage could not be lost by the addition of this evil, some imprudent persons suppose that this is not an added evil, but something which appertains to the original good. A distinction, however, occurs not only to subtle reason, but even to the most ordinary natural judgment, which was both apparent in the case of the first man and woman, and also holds good still in the case of married persons to-day. What they afterward effected in propagation, —that is the good of marriage; but what they first veiled through shame, —that is the evil of concupiscence, which everywhere shuns sight, and in its shame seeks privacy. Since, therefore, marriage effects some good even out of that evil, it has whereof to glory; but since the good cannot be affected without the evil, it has reason for feeling shame. The case may be illustrated by the example of a lame man. Suppose him to attain to some good object by limping after it, then, on the one hand, the attainment itself is not evil because of the evil of the man's lameness; nor, on the other hand, is the lameness good because of the goodness of the attainment. So, on the same principle, we ought not to condemn marriage because of the evil of lust; nor must we praise lust because of the good of marriage.

Chapter 9 [VIII.]—This Disease of Concupiscence in Marriage is Not to Be a Matter of Will, But of Necessity; What Ought to Be the Will of Believers in the Use of Matrimony; Who is to Be Regarded as Using, and Not Succumbing To, the Evil of Concupiscence; How the Holy Fathers of the Old Testament Formerly Used Wives.

This disease of concupiscence is what the apostle refers to, when, speaking to married believers, he says: "This is the will of God, even your sanctification, that ye should abstain from fornication: that every one of you should know how to possess his vessel in sanctification and honor; not in the disease of desire, even as the Gentiles which know not God." The married believer, therefore, must not only not use another man's vessel, which is what they do who lust after others' wives; but he must know that even his own vessel is not to be possessed in the disease of carnal concupiscence. And this counsel is not to be understood as if the apostle prohibited conjugal—that is to say, lawful and honorable—cohabitation; but so as that that cohabitation (which would have no adjunct of unwholesome lust, were it not that man's perfect freedom of choice had become by preceding sin so disabled that it has this fatal adjunct) should not be a matter of will, but of necessity, without which, nevertheless, it would be impossible to attain to the fruition of the will itself in the procreation of children. And this wish is not in the marriages of believers determined by the purpose of having such children born as shall pass through life in this present world, but such as shall be born again in Christ, and remain in Him for evermore. Now if this result should come about, the reward of a full felicity will spring from marriage; but if such result be not realized, there will yet ensue to the married pair the peace of their good will. Whosoever possesses his vessel (that is, his wife) with this intention of heart, certainly does not possess her in the "disease of desire," as the Gentiles which know not God, but in sanctification and honor, as believers who hope in God. A man turns to use the evil of concupiscence, and is not overcome by it, when he bridles and restrains its rage, as it works in inordinate and indecorous motions; and never relaxes his hold upon it except when intent on offspring, and then controls and applies it to the carnal generation of children to be spiritually regenerated, not to the subjection of the spirit to the flesh in a sordid servitude. That the holy fathers of olden times after Abraham, and before him, to whom God gave His testimony that "they pleased Him," thus used their wives, no one who is a Christian ought to doubt, since it was permitted to certain individuals amongst them to have a plurality of wives, where the reason was for the multiplication of their offspring, not the desire of varying gratification.

Chapter 10 [IX.]—Why It Was Sometimes Permitted that a Man Should Have Several Wives, Yet No Woman Was Ever Allowed to Have More Than One Husband. Nature Prefers Singleness in Her Dominations.

Now, if to the God of our fathers, who is likewise our God, such a plurality of wives had not been displeasing for the purpose that lust might have a fuller range of indulgence; then, on such a supposition, the holy women also ought each to have rendered service to several husbands. But if any woman had so acted, what feeling but that of a disgraceful concupiscence could impel her to have more husbands, seeing that by such license she could not have more children? That the good purpose of marriage, however, is better promoted by one husband with one wife, than by a husband with several wives, is shown plainly enough by the very first union of a married pair, which was made by the Divine Being Himself, with the intention of marriages taking their beginning therefrom, and of its affording to them a more honorable precedent. In the advance, however, of the human race, it came to pass that to certain good men were united a plurality of good wives, —many to each; and from this it would seem that moderation sought rather unity on one side for dignity, while nature permitted plurality on the other side for fecundity. For on natural principles it is more feasible for one to have dominion over many, than for many to have dominion over one. Nor can it be doubted, that it is more consonant with the order of nature that men should bear rule over women, than women over men. It is with this principle in view that the apostle says, "The head of the woman is the man;" and, "Wives, submit yourselves unto your own husbands." So also the Apostle Peter writes: "Even as Sara obeyed Abraham, calling him lord." Now, although the fact of the matter is, that while nature loves singleness in her dominations, but we may see plurality existing more readily in the subordinate portion of our race; yet for all that, it was at no time lawful for one man to have a plurality of wives, except for the purpose of a greater number of children springing from him. Wherefore, if one woman cohabits with several men, since no increase of offspring accrues to her therefrom, but only a more frequent gratification of lust, she cannot possibly be a wife, but only a harlot.

Chapter 11 [X.]—The Sacrament of Marriage; Marriage Indissoluble; The World's Law About Divorce Different from the Gospel's.

It is certainly not fecundity only, the fruit of which consists of offspring, nor chastity only, whose bond is fidelity, but also a certain sacramental bond in marriage which is recommended to believers in wedlock. Accordingly, it is enjoined by the apostle: "Husbands, love your wives, even as Christ also loved the Church." Of this bond the substance undoubtedly is this, that the man and the woman who are joined together in matrimony should remain inseparable as long as they live; and that it should be unlawful for one consort to be parted from the other, except for the cause of fornication. For this is preserved in the case of Christ and the Church; so that, as a living one with a living one, there is no divorce, no separation forever. And so complete is the observance of this bond in the city of our God, in His holy mountain—that is to say, in the Church of Christ—by all married believers, who are undoubtedly members of Christ, that, although women marry, and men take wives, for the purpose of procreating children, it is never permitted one to put away even an unfruitful wife for the sake of having another to bear children. And whosoever does this is held to be guilty of adultery by the law of the gospel; though not by this world's rule, which allows a divorce between the parties, without even the allegation of guilt, and the contraction of other nuptial engagements, —a concession which, the Lord tells us, even the holy Moses extended to the people of Israel, because of the hardness of their hearts. The same condemnation applies to the woman, if she is married to another man. So enduring, indeed, are the rights of marriage between those who have contracted them, as long as they both live, that even they are looked on as man and wife still, who have separated from one another, rather than they between whom a new connection has been formed. For by this new connection they would not be guilty of adultery, if the previous matrimonial relation did not still continue. If the husband dies, with whom a true marriage was made, a true marriage is now possible by a connection which would before have been adultery. Thus between the conjugal pair, as long as they live, the nuptial bond has a permanent obligation, and can be cancelled neither by separation nor by union with another. But this permanence avails, in such cases, only for injury from the sin, not for a bond of the covenant. In like manner the soul of an apostate, which renounces as it were its marriage union with Christ, does not, even though it has cast its faith away, lose the sacrament of its faith, which it received in the laver of regeneration. It would undoubtedly be given back to him if he were to return, although he lost it on his departure from Christ. He retains, however, the sacrament after his apostasy, to the aggravation of his punishment, not for meriting the reward.

Chapter 12 [XI.]—Marriage Does Not Cancel a Mutual Vow of Continence; There Was True Wedlock Between Mary and Joseph; In What Way Joseph Was the Father of Christ.

But God forbid that the nuptial bond should be regarded as broken between those who have by mutual consent agreed to observe a perpetual abstinence from the use of carnal concupiscence. Nay, it will be only a firmer one, whereby they have exchanged pledges together, which will have to be kept by an especial endearment and concord, —not by the voluptuous links of bodies, but by the voluntary affections of souls. For it was not deceitfully that the angel said to Joseph: "Fear not to take unto thee Mary thy wife." She is called his wife because of her first troth of betrothal, although he had had no carnal knowledge of her, nor was destined to have. The designation of wife was neither destroyed nor made untrue, where there never had been, nor was meant to be, any carnal connection. That virgin wife was rather a holier and more wonderful joy to her husband because of her very pregnancy without man, with disparity as to the child that was born, without disparity in the faith they cherished. And because of this conjugal fidelity they are both deservedly called "parents" of Christ (not only she as His mother, but he as His father, as being her husband), both having been such in mind and purpose, though not in the flesh. But while the one was His father in purpose only, and the other His mother in the flesh also, they were both of them, for all that, only the parents of His humility, not of His sublimity; of His weakness, not of His divinity. For the Gospel does not lie, in which one reads, "Both His father and His mother marveled at those things which were spoken about Him;" and in another passage, "Now His parents went to Jerusalem every year;" and again a little afterwards, "His mother said unto Him, Son, why hast Thou thus dealt with us? Behold, Thy father and I have sought Thee sorrowing." In order, however, that He might show them that He had a Father besides them, who begat Him without a mother, He said to them in answer: "How is it that ye sought me? Wist ye not that I must be about my Father's business?" Furthermore, lest He should be thought to have repudiated them as His parents by what He had just said, the evangelist at once added: "And they understood not the saying which He spoke unto them; and He went down with them, and came to Nazareth, and was subject unto them." Subject to whom but His parents? And who was the subject but Jesus Christ, "who, being in the form of God, thought it not robbery to be equal with God"? And wherefore subject to them, who were far beneath the form of God, except that "He emptied Himself, and took upon Him the form of a servant,"—the form in which His parents lived? Now, since she bore Him without his engendering, they could not surely have both been His parents, of that form of a servant, if they had not been conjugally united, though without carnal connection. Accordingly, the genealogical series (although both parents of Christ are mentioned together in the succession) had to be extended, as it is in fact, down rather to Joseph's name, that no wrong might be done, in the case of this marriage, to the male, and indeed the stronger sex, while at the same time there was nothing detrimental to truth, since Joseph, no less than Mary, was of the seed of David, of whom it was foretold that Christ should come.

Chapter 13. —In the Marriage of Mary and Joseph There Were All the Blessings of the Wedded State; All that is Born of Concubinage is Sinful Flesh.

The entire good, therefore, of the nuptial institution was affected in the case of these parents of Christ: there was offspring, there was faithfulness, there was the bond. As offspring, we recognize the Lord Jesus Himself; the fidelity, in that there was no adultery; the bond, because there was no divorce. [XII.] Only there was no nuptial cohabitation; because He who was to be without sin, and was sent not in sinful flesh, but in the likeness of sinful flesh, could not possibly have been made in sinful flesh itself without that shameful lust of the flesh which comes from sin, and without which He willed to be born, in order that He might teach us, that everyone who is born of sexual intercourse is in fact sinful flesh, since that alone which was not born of such intercourse was not sinful flesh. Nevertheless, conjugal intercourse is not in itself sin, when it is had with the intention of producing children; because the mind's good-will leads the ensuing bodily pleasure, instead of following its lead; and the human choice is not distracted by the yoke of sin pressing upon it, since the blow of the sin is rightly brought back to the purposes of procreation. This blow has a certain prurient activity which plays the king in the foul indulgences of adultery, and fornication, and lasciviousness, and uncleanness; whilst in the indispensable duties of the marriage state, it exhibits the docility of the slave. In the one case it is condemned as the shameless effrontery of so violent a master; in the other, it gets modest praise as the honest service of so submissive an attendant. This lust, then, is not in itself the good of the nuptial institution; but it is obscenity in sinful men, a necessity in procreant parents, the fire of lascivious indulgences, the shame of nuptial pleasures. Wherefore, then, may not persons remain man and wife when they cease by mutual consent from cohabitation; seeing that Joseph and Mary continued such, though they never even began to cohabit?

Chapter 14 [XIII.]—Before Christ It Was a Time for Marrying; Since Christ It Has Been a Time for Continence.

Now this propagation of children which among the ancient saints was a most bounden duty for the purpose of begetting and preserving a people for God, amongst whom the prophecy of Christ's coming must needs have had precedence over everything, now has no longer the same necessity. For from among all nations the way is open for an abundant offspring to receive spiritual regeneration, from whatever quarter they derive their natural birth. So that we may acknowledge that the scripture which says there is "a time to embrace, and a time to refrain from embracing," is to be distributed in its clauses to the periods before Christ and since. The former was the time to embrace, the latter to refrain from embracing.

Chapter 15. —The Teaching of the Apostle on This Subject.

Accordingly the apostle also, speaking apparently with this passage in view, declares: "But this I say, brethren, the time is short: it remained, that both they that have wives be as though they had them not; and they that weep, as though they wept not; and they that rejoice, as though they rejoiced not; and they that buy, as though they possessed not; and they that use this world, as though they used it not: for the fashion of this world passes away. But I would have you without solicitude." This entire passage (that I may express my view on this subject in the shape of a brief exposition of the apostle's words) I think must be understood as follows: "This I say, brethren, the time is short." No longer is God's people to be propagated by carnal generation; but, henceforth, it is to be gathered out by spiritual regeneration. "It remained, therefore, that they that have wives" be not subject to carnal concupiscence; "and they that weep," under the sadness of present evil, should rejoice in the hope of future blessing; "and they that rejoice," over any temporary advantage, should fear the eternal judgment; "and they that buy," should so hold their possessions as not to cleave to them by overmuch love; "and they that use this world" should reflect that it is passing away, and does not remain. "For the fashion of this world passes away: but," he says, "I would have you to be without solicitude,"—in other words: I would have you lift up your heart, that it may dwell among those things which do not pass away. He then goes on to say: "He that is unmarried cares for the things that belong to the Lord, how he may please the

Lord: but he that is married cares for the things that are of the world, how he may please his wife." And thus to some extent he explains what he had already said: "Let them that have wives be as though they had none." For they who have wives in such a way as to care for the things of the Lord, how they may please the Lord, without having any care for the things of the world in order to please their wives, are, in fact, just as if they had no wives. And this is affected with greater ease when the wives, too, are of such a disposition, because they please their husbands not merely because they are rich, because they are high in rank, noble in race, and amiable in natural temper, but because they are believers, because they are religious, because they are chaste, because they are good men.

Chapter 16 [XIV.]—A Certain Degree of Intemperance is to Be Tolerated in the Case of Married Persons; The Use of Matrimony for the Mere Pleasure of Lust is Not Without Sin, But Because of the Nuptial Relation the Sin is Venial.

But in the married, as these things are desirable and praiseworthy, so the others are to be tolerated, that no lapse occur into damnable sins; that is, into fornications and adulteries. To escape this evil, even such embraces of husband and wife as have not procreation for their object, but serve an overbearing concupiscence, are permitted, so far as to be within range of forgiveness, though not prescribed by way of commandment: and the married pair are enjoined not to defraud one the other, lest Satan should tempt them because of their incontinence. For thus says the Scripture: "Let the husband render unto the wife her due: and likewise, also the wife unto the husband. The wife hath not power of her own body, but the husband: and likewise, also the husband hath not power of his own body, but the wife. Defraud ye not one the other; except it be with consent for a time, that ye may have leisure for prayer; and then come together again, that Satan tempt you not for your incontinency. But I speak this by permission, and not of commandment." Now in a case where permission must be given, it cannot by any means be contended that there is not some amount of sin. Since, however, the cohabitation for the purpose of procreating children, which must be admitted being the proper end of marriage, is not sinful, what is it which the apostle allows to be permissible, but that married persons, when they have not the gift of continence, may require one from the other the due of the flesh—and that not from a wish for procreation, but for the pleasure of concupiscence? This gratification incurs not the imputation of guilt because marriage, but receives permission because marriage. This, therefore, must be reckoned among the praises of matrimony; that, on its own account, it makes pardonable that which does not essentially appertain to itself. For the nuptial embrace, which subserves the demands of concupiscence, is so affected as not to impede the child-bearing, which is the end and aim of marriage.

Chapter 17 [XV.]—What is Sinless in the Use of Matrimony? What is Attended With Venial Sin, and What with Mortal?

It is, however, one thing for married persons to have intercourse only for the wish to beget children, which is not sinful: it is another thing for them to desire carnal pleasure in cohabitation, but with the spouse only, which involves venial sin. For although propagation of offspring is not the motive of the intercourse, there is still no attempt to prevent such propagation, either by wrong desire or evil appliance. They who resort to these, although called by the name of spouses, are really not such; they retain no vestige of true matrimony, but pretend the honorable designation as a cloak for criminal conduct. Having also proceeded so far, they are betrayed into exposing their children, which are born against their will. They hate to nourish and retain those whom they were afraid they would beget. This infliction of cruelty on their offspring so reluctantly begotten, unmasks the sin which they had practiced in darkness, and drags it clearly into the light of day. The open cruelty reproves the concealed sin. Sometimes, indeed, this lustful cruelty, or, if you please, cruel lust, resorts to such extravagant methods as to use poisonous drugs to secure barrenness; or else, if unsuccessful in this, to destroy the conceived seed by some means before birth, preferring that its offspring should rather perish than receive vitality; or if it was advancing to life within the womb, should be slain before it was born. Well, if both parties alike are so flagitious, they are not husband and wife; and if such were their character from the beginning, they have not come together by wedlock but by debauchery. But if the two are not alike in such sin, I boldly declare either that the woman is, so to say, the husband's harlot; or the man the wife's adulterer.

Chapter 18 [XVI.]—Continence Better Than

Marriage; But Marriage Better Than Fornication.

Forasmuch, then, as marriage cannot be such as that of the primitive men might have been, if sin had not preceded; it may yet be like that of the holy fathers of the olden time, in such wise that the carnal concupiscence which causes shame (which did not exist in paradise previous to the fall, and after that event was not allowed to remain there), although necessarily forming a part of the body of this death, is not subservient to it, but only submits its function, when forced thereto, for the sole purpose of assisting in the procreation of children; otherwise, since the present time (as we have already said) is the period for abstaining from the nuptial embrace, and therefore makes no necessary demand on the exercise of the said function, seeing that all nations now contribute so abundantly to the production of an offspring which shall receive spiritual birth, there is the greater room for the blessing of an excellent continence. "He that is able to receive it, let him receive it." He, however, who cannot receive it, "even if he marry, sinned not;" and if a woman have not the gift of continence, let her also marry. "It is good, indeed, for a man not to touch a woman." But since "all men cannot receive this saying, save they to whom it is given," it remains that "to avoid fornication, every man ought to have his own wife, and every woman her own husband." And thus the weakness of incontinence is hindered from falling into the ruin of profligacy by the honorable estate of matrimony. Now that which the apostle says of women, "I will therefore that the younger women marry," is also applicable to males: I will that the younger men take wives; that so it may appertain to both sexes alike "to bear children, to be" fathers and "mothers of families, to give none occasion to the adversary to speak reproachfully."

### Chapter 19 [XVII.]—Blessing of Matrimony.

In matrimony, however, let these nuptial blessings be the objects of our love—offspring, fidelity, the sacramental bond. Offspring, not that it be born only, but born again; for it is born to punishment unless it be born again to life. Fidelity, not such as even unbelievers observe one towards the other, in their ardent love of the flesh. For what husband, however impious himself, likes an adulterous wife? Or what wife, however impious she be, likes an adulterous husband? This is indeed a natural good in marriage, though a carnal one. But a member of Christ ought to be afraid of adultery, not because himself, but of his spouse; and ought to hope to receive from Christ the reward of that fidelity which he shows to his spouse. The sacramental bond, again, which is lost neither by divorce nor by adultery, should be guarded by husband and wife with concord and chastity. For it alone is that which even an unfruitful marriage retains by the law of piety, now that all that hope of fruitfulness is lost for the purpose of which the couple married. Let these nuptial blessings be praised in marriage by him who wishes to extol the nuptial institution. Carnal concupiscence, however, must not be ascribed to marriage: it is only to be tolerated in marriage. It is not a good which comes out of the essence of marriage, but an evil which is the accident of original sin.

### Chapter 20 [XVIII]—Why Children of Wrath are Born of Holy Matrimony.

This is the reason, indeed, why of even the just and lawful marriages of the children of God are born, not children of God, but children of the world; because also those who generate, if they are already regenerate, beget children not as children of God, but as still children of the world. "The children of this world," says our Lord, "beget and are begotten." From the fact, therefore, that we are still children of this world, our outer man is in a state of corruption; and on this account our offspring are born as children of the present world; nor do they become sons of God, except they be regenerated. Yet since we are children of God, our inner man is renewed from day to day. And yet even our outer man has been sanctified through the laver of regeneration, and has received the hope of future incorruption, on which account it is justly designated as "the temple of God." "Your bodies," says the apostle, "are the temples of the Holy Ghost, which is in you, and which ye have of God; and ye are not your own, for ye are bought with a great price: therefore, glorify and carry God in your body." The whole of this statement is made about our present sanctification, but especially in consequence of that hope of which he says in another passage, "We ourselves also, which have the first-fruits of the Spirit, even we ourselves groan within ourselves, waiting for the adoption, to wit, the redemption of our body." If, then, the redemption of our body is expected, as the apostle declares, it follows, that being an expectation, it is as yet a matter of hope, and not of actual possession. Accordingly the apostle adds: "For we are saved by hope: but hope that is seen is not hope: for what a man sees, why doth he yet hope for? But if we hope for that we see not, then do we with patience wait for it." Not, therefore, by that which we are waiting for, but by that which we are now enduring, are the children of our flesh born. God forbid that a man who possesses faith should, when he hears the apostle bid men "love their wives," love that carnal concupiscence in his wife which he ought not to love even in himself; as he may know, if he listens to the words of another apostle: "Love not the world, neither the things that are in the world. If any man love the world, the love of the Father is not in him. For all that is in the world, the lust of the flesh, and the lust of the eyes, and the pride of life, is not of the Father, but is of the world. And the world passes away, and the lust thereof: but he that doeth the will of God abides forever, even as also God abides forever."

Chapter 21 [XIX.]—Thus Sinners are Born of Righteous Parents, Even as Wild Olives Spring from the Olive.

That, therefore, which is born of the lust of the flesh is really born of the world, and not of God; but it is born of God, when it is born again of water and of the Spirit. The guilt of this concupiscence, regeneration alone remits, even as natural generation contracts it. What, then, is generated must be regenerated, in order that likewise since it cannot be otherwise, what has been contracted may be remitted. It is, no doubt, very wonderful that what has been remitted in the parent should still be contracted in the offspring; but nevertheless such is the case. That this mysterious verity, which unbelievers neither see nor believe, might get some palpable evidence in its support, God in His providence has secured in the example of certain trees. For why should we not suppose that for this very purpose the wild olive springs from the olive? Is it not indeed credible that, in a thing which has been created for the use of mankind, the Creator provided and appointed what should afford an instructive example, applicable to the human race? It is a wonderful thing, then, how those who have been themselves delivered by grace from the bondage of sin, should still beget those who are tied and bound by the self-same chain, and who require the same process of loosening? Yes; and we admit the wonderful fact. But that the embryo of wild olive trees should latently exist in the germs of true olives, who would deem credible, if it were not proved true by experiment and observation? In the same manner, therefore, as a wild olive grows out of the seed of the wild olive, and from the seed of the true olive springs also nothing but a wild olive, notwithstanding the very great difference there is between the wild olive and the olive; so what is born in the flesh, either of a sinner or of a just man, is in both instances a sinner, notwithstanding the vast distinction which exists between the sinner and the righteous man. He that is begotten is no sinner as yet in act, and is still new from his birth; but in guilt he is old. Human from the Creator, he is a captive of the destroyer, and needs a redeemer. The difficulty, however, is how a state of captivity can possibly befall the offspring, when the parents have been themselves previously redeemed from it. Now it is no easy matter to unravel this intricate point, or to explain it in a set discourse; therefore unbelievers refuse to accept it as true; just as if in that other point about the wild olive and the olive, which we gave in illustration, any reason could be easily found, or explanation clearly given, why the self-same shoot should sprout out of so dissimilar a stock. The truth, however, of this can be discovered by anyone who is willing to make the experiment. Let it then serve for a good example for suggesting belief of what admits not of ocular demonstration.

Chapter 22 [XX.]—Even Infants, When Unbaptized, are in the Power of the Devil; Exorcism in the Case of Infants, and Renunciation of the Devil.

Now the Christian faith unfalteringly declares, what our new heretics have begun to deny, both that they who are cleansed in the laver of regeneration are redeemed from the power of the devil, and that those who have not yet been redeemed by such regeneration are still captive in the power of the devil, even if they be infant children of the redeemed, unless they be themselves redeemed by the self-same grace of Christ. For we cannot doubt that that blessing of God applies to every stage of human life, which the apostle describes when he says concerning Him: "Who hath delivered us from the power of darkness, and hath translated us into the kingdom of His dear Son." From this power of darkness, therefore, of which the devil is the prince, —in other words, from the power of the devil and his angels, —infants are delivered when they are baptized; and whosoever denies this, is convicted by the truth of the Church's very sacraments, which no heretical novelty in the Church of Christ is permitted to destroy or change, so long as the Divine Head rules and helps the entire body which He owns— small as well as great. It is true, then, and in no way false, that the devil's power is exorcised in infants, and that they renounce him by the hearts and mouths of those who bring them to baptism, being unable to do so by their own; in order that they may be delivered from the power of darkness, and be translated into the kingdom of their Lord. What is that, therefore, within them which keeps them in the power of the devil until they are delivered from it by Christ's sacrament of baptism? What is it, I ask, but sin? Nothing else, indeed, has the devil found which enables him to put under his own control that nature of man which the good Creator made good. But infants have committed no sin of their own since they have been alive. Only original sin, therefore, remains, whereby they are made captive under the devil's power, until they are redeemed therefrom by the laver of regeneration and the blood of Christ, and pass into their Redeemer's kingdom, —the power of their enthraller being frustrated, and power being given them to become "sons of God" instead of children of this world.

Chapter 23 [XXI.]—Sin Has Not Arisen Out of the Goodness of Marriage; The Sacrament of Matrimony a Great One in the Case of Christ and the Church—A Very Small One in the Case of a Man and His Wife.

If now we interrogate, so to speak, those goods of marriage to which we have often referred, and inquire how it is that sin could possibly have been propagated from them to infants, we shall get this answer from the first of them—the work of procreation of offspring: "My happiness would in paradise have been greater if sin had not been committed. For to me belongs that blessing of almighty God: 'Be fruitful, and multiply.' For accomplishing this good work, divers members were created suited to each sex; these members were, of course, in existence before sin, but they were not objects of shame." This will be the answer of the second good—the fidelity of chastity: "If sin had not been committed, what in paradise could have been more secure than myself, when there was no lust of my own to spur me, none of another to tempt me?" And then this will be the answer of the sacramental bond of marriage, —the third good: "Of me was that word spoken in paradise before the entrance of sin: 'A man shall leave his father and his mother, and shall cleave unto his wife; and they two shall become one flesh.'" This the apostle applies to the case of Christ and of the Church, and calls it then "a great sacrament." What, then, in Christ and in the Church is great, in the instances of each married pair it is but very small, but even then it is the sacrament of an inseparable union. What now is there in these three blessings of marriage out of which the bond of sin could pass over to posterity? Absolutely nothing. And in these blessings it is certain that the goodness of matrimony is entirely comprised; and even now good wedlock consists of these same blessings.

Chapter 24. —Lust and Shame Come from Sin; The Law of Sin; The Shamelessness of the Cynics.

But if, in like manner, the question be asked of the concupiscence of the flesh, how it is that acts now bring shame which once were free from shame, will not her answer be, that she only began to have existence in men's members after sin? [XXII.] And, therefore, that the apostle designated her influence as "the law of sin," inasmuch as she subjugated man to herself when he was unwilling to remain subject to his God; and that it was she who made the first married pair ashamed at that moment when they covered their loins; even as all are still ashamed, and seek out secret retreats for cohabitation, and dare not have even the children, whom they have themselves thus begotten, to be witnesses of what they do. It was against this modesty of natural shame that the Cynic philosophers, in the error of their astonishing shamelessness, struggled so hard: they thought that the intercourse indeed of husband and wife, since it was lawful and honorable, should therefore be done in public. Such barefaced obscenity deserved to receive the name of dogs; and so they went by the title of "Cynics."

Chapter 25 [XXIII.]—Concupiscence in the Regenerate Without Consent is Not Sin; In What Sense Concupiscence is Called Sin.

Now this concupiscence, this law of sin which dwells in our members, to which the law of righteousness forbids allegiance, saying in the words of the apostle, "Let not sin, therefore, reign in your mortal body, that ye should obey it in the lusts thereof; neither yield ye your members as instruments of unrighteousness unto sin:"— this concupiscence, I say, which is cleansed only by the sacrament of regeneration, does undoubtedly, by means of natural birth, pass on the bond of sin to a man's posterity, unless they are themselves loosed from it by regeneration. In the case, however, of the regenerate, concupiscence is not itself sin any longer, whenever they do not consent to it for illicit works, and when the members are not applied by the presiding mind to perpetrate such deeds. So that, if what is enjoined in one passage, "Thou shalt not covet," is not kept, that at any rate is observed which is commanded in another place, "Thou shalt not go after thy concupiscences." Inasmuch, however, as by a certain manner of speech it is called sin, since it arose from sin, and, when it has the upper hand, produces sin, the guilt of it prevails in the natural man; but this guilt, by Christ's grace through the remission of all sins, is not suffered to prevail in the regenerate man, if he does not yield obedience to it whenever it urges him to the commission of evil. As arising from sin, it is, I say, called sin, although in the regenerate it is not actually sin; and it has this designation applied to it, just as speech which the tongue produces is itself called "tongue;" and just as the word "hand" is used in the sense of writing, which the hand produces. In the same way concupiscence is called sin, as producing sin when it conquers the will: so to cold and frost the epithet "sluggish" is given; not as arising from, but as productive of, sluggishness; benumbing us, in fact.

Chapter 26. —Whatever is Born Through Concupiscence is Not Undeservedly in Subjection to the Devil by Reason of Sin; The Devil Deserves Heavier Punishment Than Men.

This wound which the devil has inflicted on the human race compels everything which has its birth in consequence of it to be under the devil's power, as if he were rightly plucking fruit off his own tree. Not as if man's nature, which is only of God, came from him, but sin alone, which is not of God. For it is not on its own account that man's nature is under condemnation, because it is the work of God, and therefore laudable; but because that condemnable corruption by which it has been vitiated. Now it is because of this condemnation that it is in subjection to the devil, who is also in the same damnable state. For the devil is himself an unclean spirit: good, indeed, so far as he is a spirit, but evil as being unclean; for by nature he is a spirit, by the corruption thereof an unclean one. Of these two, the one is of God, the other of himself. His hold over men, therefore, whether of an advanced age or in infancy, is not because they are human, but because they are polluted. He, then, who feels surprise that God's creature is a subject of the devil, should cease from such feeling. For one creature of God is in subjection to another creature of God, the less to the greater, a human being to an angelic one; and this is not owing to nature, but to a corruption of nature: polluted is the sovereign, polluted also the subject. All this is the fruit of that ancient stock of pollution which he has planted in man; himself being destined to suffer a heavier punishment at the last judgment, as being the more polluted; but at the same time even they who will have to bear a less heavy burden in that condemnation are subjects of him as the prince and author of sin, for there will be no other cause of condemnation than sin.

Chapter 27 [XXIV.]—Through Lust Original Sin is Transmitted; Venial Sins in Married Persons; Concupiscence of the Flesh, the Daughter and Mother of Sin.

Wherefore the devil holds infants guilty who are born, not of the good by which marriage is good, but of the evil of concupiscence, which, indeed, marriage uses aright, but at which even marriage has occasion to feel shame. Marriage is itself "honorable in all" the goods which properly appertain to it; but even when it has its "bed undefiled" (not only by fornication and adultery, which are damnable disgraces, but also by any of those excesses of cohabitation such as do not arise from any prevailing desire of children, but from an overbearing lust of pleasure, which are venial sins in man and wife), yet, whenever it comes to the actual process of generation, the very embrace which is lawful and honorable cannot be effected without the ardor of lust, so as to be able to accomplish that which appertains to the use of reason and not of lust. Now, this ardor, whether following or preceding the will, does somehow, by a power of its own, move the members which cannot be moved simply by the will, and in this manner it shows itself not to be the servant of a will which commands it, but rather to be the punishment of a will which disobeys it. It shows, moreover, that it must be excited, not by a free choice, but by a certain seductive stimulus, and that on this very account it produces shame. This is the carnal concupiscence, which, while it is no longer accounted sin in the regenerate, yet in no case happens to nature except from sin. It is the daughter of sin, as it were; and whenever it yields assent to the commission of shameful deeds, it becomes also the mother of many sins. Now from this concupiscence whatever comes into being by natural birth is bound by original sin, unless, indeed, it be born again in Him whom the Virgin conceived without this concupiscence. Wherefore, when He vouchsafed to be born in the flesh, He alone was born without sin.

Chapter 28 [XXV.]—Concupiscence Remains After Baptism, Just as Languor Does After Recovery from Disease; Concupiscence is Diminished in Persons of Advancing Years, and Increased in the Incontinent.

If the question arises, how this concupiscence of the flesh remains in the regenerate, in whose case has been effected a remission of all sins whatever; seeing that human semination takes place by its means, even when the carnal offspring of even a baptized parent is born: or, at all events, if it may be in the case of a baptized parent concupiscence and not be sin, why should this same concupiscence be sin in the offspring?—the answer to be given is this: Carnal concupiscence is remitted, indeed, in baptism; not so that it is put out of existence, but so that it is not to be imputed for sin. Although its guilt is now taken away, it still remains until our entire infirmity be healed by the advancing renewal of our inner man, day by day, when at last our outward man shall be clothed with incorruption. It does not remain, however, substantially, as a body, or a spirit; but it is nothing more than a certain affection of an evil quality, such as languor, for instance. There is not, to be sure, anything remaining which may be remitted whenever, as the Scripture says, "the Lord forgives all our iniquities." But until that happens which immediately follows in the same passage, "Who heals all thine infirmities, who redeems thy life from corruption," there remains this concupiscence of the flesh in the body of this death. Now we are admonished not to obey its sinful desires to do evil: "Let not sin reign in your mortal body." Still this concupiscence is daily lessened in persons of continence and increasing years, and most of all when old age makes a near approach. The man, however, who yields to it a wicked service, receives such great energies that, even when all his members are now failing through age, and those especial parts of his body are unable to be applied to their proper function, he does not ever cease to revel in a still increasing rage of disgraceful and shameless desire.

Chapter 29 [XXVI.]—How Concupiscence Remains in the Baptized in Act, When It Has Passed Away as to Its Guilt.

In the case, then, of those persons who are born again in Christ, when they receive an entire remission of all their sins, it is of course necessary that the guilt also of the still indwelling concupiscence should be remitted, in order that (as I said) it should not be imputed to them for sin. For even as in the case of those sins which cannot be themselves permanent, since they pass away as soon as they are committed, the guilt yet is permanent, and (if not remitted) will remain for evermore; so, when the concupiscence is remitted, the guilt of it also is taken away. For not to have sin means this, not to be deemed guilty of sin. If a man has (for example) committed adultery, though he does not repeat the sin, he is held to be guilty of adultery until the indulgence in guilt be itself remitted. He has the sin, therefore, remaining, although the particular act of his sin no longer exists, since it has passed away along with the time when it was committed. For if to desist from sinning were the same thing as not to have sins, it would be sufficient if Scripture were content to give us the simple warning, "My son, hast thou sinned? Do so no more." This, however, does not suffice, for it goes on to say, "Ask forgiveness for thy former sins." Sins remain, therefore, if they are not forgiven. But how do they remain if they are passed away? Only thus, they have passed away in their act, but they are permanent in their guilt. Contrariwise, then, may it happen that a thing may remain in act, but pass away in guilt.

Chapter 30 [XXVII.]—The Evil Desires of Concupiscence; We Ought to Wish that They May Not Be.

For the concupiscence of the flesh is in some sort active, even when it does not exhibit either an assent of the heart, where its seat of empire is, or those members whereby, as its weapons, it fulfils what it is bent on. But what in this action does it effect, unless it be its evil and shameful desires? For if these were good and lawful, the apostle would not forbid obedience to them, saying, "Let not sin therefore reign in your mortal body, that ye should obey the lusts thereof." He does not say, that ye should have the lusts thereof, but "that ye should obey the lusts thereof;" in order that (as these desires are greater or less in different individuals, according as each shall have progressed in the renewal of the inner man) we may maintain the fight of holiness and chastity, for the purpose of withholding obedience to these lusts. Nevertheless, our wish ought to be nothing less than the nonexistence of these very desires, even if the accomplishment of such a wish be not possible in the body of this death. This is the reason why the same apostle, in another passage, addressing us as if in his own person, gives us this instruction: "For what I would," says he, "that do I not; but what I hate, that do I." In a word, "I covet." For he was unwilling to do this, that he might be perfect on every side. "If, then, I do that which I would not," he goes on to say, "I consent unto the law that it is good." Because the law, too, wills not that which I also would not. For it wills not that I should have concupiscence, for it says, "Thou shall not covet;" and I am no less unwilling to cherish so evil a desire. In this, therefore, there is complete accord between the will of the law and my own will. But because he was unwilling to covet, and yet did covet, and for all that did not by any means obey this concupiscence so as to yield assent to it, he immediately adds these words: "Now, then, it is no more I that do it, but sin that dwelleth in me."

Chapter 31 [XXVIII.]—Who is the Man that Can Say, "It is No More I that Do It"?

A man, however, is much deceived if, while consenting to the lust of his flesh, and then both resolving in his mind to do its desires and setting about it, he supposes that he has still a right to say, "It is not I that do it," even if he hates and loathes himself for assenting to evil desires. The two things are simultaneous in his case: he hates the thing himself because he knows that it is evil; and yet he does it, because he is bent on doing it. Now if, in addition to all this, he proceeds to do what the Scripture forbids him, when it says, "Neither yield ye your members as instruments of unrighteousness unto sin," and completes with a bodily act what he was bent on doing in his mind; and says, "It is not I that do the thing, but sin that dwelleth in me," because he feels displeased with himself for resolving on and accomplishing the deed, — he so greatly errs as not to know his own self. For, whereas he is altogether himself, his mind determining and his body executing his own purpose, he yet supposes that he is himself no longer! [XXIX.] That man, therefore, alone speaks the truth when he says, "It is no more I that do it, but sin that dwelleth in me," who only feels the concupiscence, and neither resolves on doing it with the consent of his heart, nor accomplishes it with the ministry of his body.

Chapter 32. —When Good Will Be Perfectly Done.

The apostle then adds these words: "For I know that in me (that is, in my flesh) dwelleth no good thing: for to will is present with me; but how to perfect that which is good I find not." Now this is said, because a good thing is not then perfected, when there is an absence of evil desires, as evil is perfected when evil desires are obeyed. But when they are present, but are not obeyed, neither evil is performed, since obedience is not yielded to them; nor good, because of their inoperative presence. There is rather an intermediate condition of things: good is affected in some degree, because the evil concupiscence has gained no assent to itself; and in some degree there is a remnant of evil, because the concupiscence is present. This accounts for the apostle's precise words. He does not say, To do good is not present to him, but "how to perfect it." For the truth is, one does a good deal of good when he does what the Scripture enjoins, "Go not after thy lusts;" yet he falls short of perfection, in that he fails to keep the great commandment, "Thou shalt not covet." The law said, "Thou shalt not covet," in order that, when we find ourselves lying in this diseased state, we might seek the medicine of Grace, and by that commandment know both in what direction our endeavors should aim as we advance in our present mortal condition, and to what a height it is possible to reach in the future immortality. For unless perfection could somewhere be attained, this commandment would never have been given to us.

Chapter 33 [XXX.]—True Freedom Comes with Willing Delight in God's Law.

The apostle then repeats his former statement, the more fully to recommend its purport: "For the good," says he, "that I would, I do not: but the evil which I would not, that I do. Now, if I do that I would not, it is no more I that do it, but sin that dwelleth in me." Then follows this: "I find then the law, when I would act, to be good to me; for evil is present with me." In other words, I find that the law is a good to me, when I wish to do what the law would have me do; since it is not with the law itself (which says, "Thou shalt not covet") that evil is present; no, it is with myself that the evil is present, which I would not do, because I have the concupiscence even in my willingness. "For," he adds, "I delight in the law of God after the inward man; but I see another law in my members warring against the law of my mind, and bringing me into captivity to the law of sin which is in my members." This delight with the law of God after the inward man, comes to us from the mighty grace of God; for thereby is our inward man renewed day by day, because it is thereby that progress is made by us with perseverance. In it there is not the fear that has torment, but the love that cheers and gratifies. We are truly free there, where we have no unwilling joy.

Chapter 34. —How Concupiscence Made a Captive of the Apostle; What the Law of Sin Was to the Apostle.

Then, indeed, this statement, "I see another law in my members warring against the law of my mind," refers to that very concupiscence which we are now speaking of—the law of sin in our sinful flesh. But when he said, "And bringing me into captivity to the law of sin," that is, to its own self, "which is in my members," he either meant "bringing me into captivity," in the sense of endeavoring to make me captive, that is, urging me to approve and accomplish evil desire; or rather (and this opens no controversy), in the sense of leading me captive according to the flesh, and, if this is not possessed by the carnal concupiscence which he calls the law of sin, no unlawful desire—such as our mind ought not to obey— would, of course, be there to excite and disturb. The fact, however, that the apostle does not say, Bringing my flesh into captivity, but "Bringing me into captivity," leads us to look out for some other meaning for the phrase, and to understand the term "bringing me into captivity" as if he had said, endeavoring to make me captive. But why, after all, might he not say, "Bringing me into captivity," and at the same time mean us to understand his flesh? Was it not spoken by one concerning Jesus, when His flesh was not found in the sepulcher: "They have taken away my Lord, and I know not where they have laid Him"? Was Mary's then an improper question, because she said, "My Lord," and not "My Lord's body" or "flesh"?

Chapter 35 [XXXI.]—The Flesh, Carnal Affection.

But we have in the apostle's own language, a little before, a sufficiently clear proof that he might have meant his flesh when he said, "Bringing me into captivity." For after declaring, "I know that in me dwells no good thing," he at once added an explanatory sentence to this effect, "That is, in my flesh." It is then the flesh, in which there dwells nothing good, that is brought into captivity to the law of sin. Now he designates that as the flesh wherein lies a certain morbid carnal affection, not the mere conformation of our bodily fabric whose members are not to be used as weapons for sin—that is, for that very concupiscence which holds this flesh of ours captive. So far, indeed, as concerns this actual bodily substance and nature of ours, it is already God's temple in all faithful men, whether living in marriage or in continence. If, however, absolutely nothing of our flesh were in captivity, not even to the devil, because there has accrued to it the remission of sin, that sin be not imputed to it (and this is properly designated the law of sin); yet if under this law of sin, that is, under its own concupiscence, our flesh were not to some degree held captive, how could that be true which the apostle states, when he speaks of our "waiting for the adoption, to wit, the redemption of our body"? In so far, then, as there is now this waiting for the redemption of our body, there is also in some degree still existing something in us which is a captive to the law of sin. Accordingly he exclaims, "O wretched man that I am! who shall deliver me from the body of this death? The grace of God, through Jesus Christ our Lord." What are we to understand by such language, but that our body, which is undergoing corruption, weighs heavily on our soul? When, therefore, this very body of ours shall be restored to us in an incorrupt state, there shall be a full liberation from the body of this death; but there will be no such deliverance for them who shall rise again to condemnation. To the body of this death then is understood to be owing the circumstance that there is in our members another law which wars against the law of the mind, so long as the flesh lusts against the spirit— without, however, subjugating the mind, since on its side, too, the spirit has a concupiscence contrary to the flesh. Thus, although the actual law of sin partly holds the flesh in captivity (whence comes its resistance to the law of the mind), still it has not an absolute empire in our body, notwithstanding its mortal state, since it refuses obedience to its desires. For in the case of hostile armies between whom there is an earnest conflict, even the side which is inferior in the fight usually holds a something which it has captured; and although in some such way there is somewhat in our flesh which is kept under the law of sin, yet it has before it the hope of redemption: and then there will remain not a particle of this corrupt concupiscence; but our flesh, healed of that diseased plague, and wholly clad in immortality, shall live for evermore in eternal blessedness.

Chapter 36. —Even Now While We Still Have Concupiscence We May Be Safe in Christ.

But the apostle pursues the subject, and says, "So then with the mind I myself serve the law of God, but with the flesh the law of sin;" which must be thus understood: "With my mind I serve the law of God," by refusing my consent to the law of sin; "with my flesh, however," I serve "the law of sin," by having the desires of sin, from which I am not yet entirely freed, although I yield them no assent. Then let us observe carefully what he has said after all the above: "There is therefore now no condemnation to them which are in Christ Jesus." Even now, says he, when the law in my members keeps up its warfare against the law of my mind, and retains in captivity somewhat in the body of this death, there is no condemnation to them which are in Christ Jesus. And listen why: "For the law of the spirit of life in Christ Jesus," says he, "hath made me free from the law of sin and death." How made me free, except by abolishing its sentence of guilt by the remission of all my sins; so that, though it still remains, only daily lessening more and more, it is nevertheless not imputed to me as sin?

Chapter 37 [XXXII.]—The Law of Sin with Its Guilt in Unbaptized Infants. By Adam's Sin the Human Race Has Become a "Wild Olive Tree."

Until, then, this remission of sins takes place in the offspring, they have within them the law of sin in such manner, that it is really imputed to them as sin; in other words, with that law there is attaching to them its sentence of guilt, which holds them debtors to eternal condemnation. For what a parent transmits to his carnal offspring is the condition of his own carnal birth, not that of his spiritual new birth. For, that he was born in the flesh, although no hindrance after the remission of his guilt to his fruit, still remains hidden, as it were, in the seed of the olive, even though, because of the remission of his sins, it in no respect injures the oil—that is, in plain language, his life which he lives, "righteous by faith," after Christ, whose very name comes from the oil, that is, from the anointing. That, however, which in the case of a regenerate parent, as in the seed of the pure olive, is covered without any guilt, which has been remitted, is still no doubt retained in the case of his offspring, which is yet unregenerate, as in the wild olive, with all its guilt, until here also it be remitted by the self-same grace. When Adam sinned, he was changed from that pure olive, which had no such corrupt seed whence should spring the bitter issue of the wild olive, into a wild olive tree; and, since his sin was so great, that by it his nature became commensurately changed for the worse, he converted the entire race of man into a wild olive stock. The effect of this change we see illustrated, as has been said above, in the instance of these very trees. Whenever God's grace converts a sapling into a good olive, so that the fault of the first birth (that original sin which had been derived and contracted from the concupiscence of the flesh) is remitted, covered, and not imputed, there is still inherent in it that nature from which is born a wild olive, unless it, too, by the same grace, is by the second birth changed into a good olive.

Chapter 38 [XXXIII.]—To Baptism Must Be Referred All Remission of Sins, and the Complete Healing of the Resurrection. Daily Cleansing.

Blessed, therefore, is the olive tree "whose iniquities are forgiven, and whose sins are covered;" blessed is it "to which the Lord hath not imputed sin." But this, which has received the remission, the covering, and the acquittal, even up to the complete change into an eternal immortality, still retains a secret force which furnishes seed for a wild and bitter olive tree, unless the same tillage of God prunes it also, by remission, covering, and acquittal. There will, however, be left no corruption at all in even carnal seed, when the same regeneration, which is now affected through the sacred laver, purges and heals all man's evil to the very end. By its means the very same flesh, through which the carnal mind was formed, shall become spiritual, —no longer having that carnal lust which resists the law of the mind, no longer emitting carnal seed. For in this sense must be understood that which the apostle whom we have so often quoted says elsewhere: "Christ loved the Church, and gave Himself for it; that He might sanctify and cleanse it by the washing of water by the word; that He might present it to Himself a glorious Church, not having spot, or wrinkle, or any such thing." It must, I say, be understood as implying, that by this laver of regeneration and word of sanctification all the evils of regenerate men of whatever kind are cleansed and healed,—not the sins only which are all now remitted in baptism, but those also which after baptism are committed by human ignorance and frailty; not, indeed, that baptism is to be repeated as often as sin is repeated, but that by its one only ministration it comes to pass that pardon is secured to the faithful of all their sins both before and after their regeneration. For of what use would repentance be, either before baptism, if baptism did not follow; or after it, if it did not precede? Nay, in the Lord's Prayer itself, which is our daily cleansing, of what avail or advantage would it be for that petition to be uttered, "Forgive us our debts," unless it be by such as have been baptized? And in like manner, how great so ever be the liberality and kindness of a man's alms, what,

I ask, would they profit him towards the remission of his sins if he had not been baptized? In short, on whom but on the baptized shall be bestowed the very felicities of the kingdom of heaven; where the Church shall have no spot, or wrinkle, or any such thing; where there shall be nothing blameworthy, nothing unreal; where there shall be not only no guilt for sin, but no concupiscence to excite it?

Chapter 39 [XXXIV.]—By the Holiness of Baptism, Not Sins Only, But All Evils Whatsoever, Have to Be Removed. The Church is Not Yet Free from All Stain.

And thus not only all the sins, but all the ills of men of what kind so ever, are in course of removal by the holiness of that Christian laver whereby Christ cleanses His Church, that He may present it to Himself, not in this world, but in that which is to come, as not having spot, or wrinkle, or any such thing. Now there are some who maintain that such is the Church even now, and yet they are in it. Well then, since they confess that they have some sins themselves, if they say the truth in this (and, of course, they do, as they are not free from sins), then the Church has "a spot" in them; whilst if they tell an untruth in their confession (as speaking from a double heart), then the Church has in them "a wrinkle." If, however, they assert that it is themselves, and not the Church, which has all this, they then as good as acknowledge that they are not its members, nor belong to its body, so that they are even condemned by their own confession.

Chapter 40 [XXXV.]—Refutation of the Pelagians by the Authority of St. Ambrose, Whom They Quote to Show that the Desire of the Flesh is a Natural Good.

In respect, however, to this concupiscence of the flesh, we have striven in this lengthy discussion to distinguish it accurately from the goods of marriage. This we have done because our modern heretics, who cavil whenever concupiscence is censured, as if it involved a censure of marriage. Their object is to praise concupiscence as a natural good, that so they may defend their own baneful dogma, which asserts that those who are born by its means do not contract original sin. Now the blessed Ambrose, bishop of Milan, by whose priestly office I received the washing of regeneration, briefly spoke on this matter, when, expounding the prophet Isaiah, he gathered from him the nativity of Christ in the flesh: "Thus," says the bishop, "He was both tempted in all points as a man, and in the likeness of man He bare all things; but since He was born of the Spirit, He kept Himself from sin. For every man is a liar; and there is none without sin but God alone. It has, therefore, been ever firmly maintained, that it is clear that no man from husband and wife, that is to say, by means of that conjunction of their persons, is free from sin. He who is free from sin is also free from conception of this kind." Well now, what is it which St. Ambrose has here condemned in the true doctrine of this deliverance? —is it the goodness of marriage, or not rather the worthless opinion of these heretics, although they had not then come upon the stage? I have thought it worthwhile to adduce this testimony, because Pelagius mentions Ambrose with such commendation as to say: "The blessed Bishop

Ambrose, in whose writings more than anywhere else the Roman faith is clearly stated, has flourished like a beautiful flower among the Latin writers. His fidelity and extremely pure perception of the sense of Scripture no opponent even has ever ventured to impugn." I hope he may regret having entertained opinions opposed to Ambrose, but not that he has bestowed this praise on that holy man.

Here, then, you have my book, which, owing to its tedious length and difficult subject, it has been as troublesome for me to compose as for you to read, in those little snatches of time in which you have been able (or at least, as I suppose, have been able) to find yourself at leisure. Although it has been indeed drawn up with considerable labor amidst my ecclesiastical duties, as God has vouchsafed to give me His help, I should hardly have intruded it on your notice, with all your public cares, if I had not been informed by a godly man, who has an intimate knowledge of you, that you take such pleasure in reading as to lie awake by the hour, night after night, spending the precious time in your favorite pursuit.

PRELIMINARY NOTES ON THE SECOND BOOK.

---

(1) From the Preface of Augustin's "Unfinished Work Against Julianus."

I Wrote a treatise, under the title On Marriage and Concupiscence, and addressed it to the Count Valerius, on learning that he had been informed of the Pelagians that they charge us with condemning marriage. Now in that treatise I showed the distinction, as critically and accurately as I was able, between the good of marriage and the evil of carnal concupiscence, —an evil which is well used by conjugal chastity. On receiving my treatise, the illustrious man whom I have named sent me in a short paper a few sentences culled from a work of Julianus, a Pelagian heretic. In this work he has thought fit to extend to four books his answer to the before-mentioned treatise of mine, which is limited to one book only, On Marriage and Concupiscence. I do not know to whom we were indebted for the said extracts: he confined his selection, evidently on purpose, to the first book of Julianus' work. At the request of Valerius, I lost no time in drawing up my answer to the extracts. And thus it happened that I have written a second book also under the same title; and in reply to this Julianus has drawn up to eight books, in excess of his loquacious powers.

(2) From Augustin's Epistle to Claudius [CCVII.].

"Whoever has perused this second book of mine, addressed (as the first was) to the Count Valerius, and drawn up (as, indeed, both were) for his use, will have discovered that there are some points in which I have not answered Julianus, but that I meant my work rather for him who made the extracts from that writer's books, and who did not arrange them in the order in which he found them. He deemed some considerable alteration necessary in his arrangement, very probably with the view of appropriating by this method as his own the thoughts which evidently were another person's."

Book II.

Augustin, in this latter book, refutes sundry sentences which had been culled by some unknown author from the first of four books that Julianus had published in opposition to the former book of his treatise "On Marriage and Concupiscence;" which sentences had been forwarded to him at the instance of the Count Valerius. He vindicates the Catholic doctrine of original sin from his opponent's cavils and subtleties, and particularly shows how diverse it is from the infamous heresy of the Manicheans.

Chapter 1 [I.]—Introductory Statement.

I Cannot tell you, dearly loved and honored son Valerius, how great is the pleasure which my heart receives when I hear of your warm and earnest interest in the testimony of the word of God against the heretics; and this, too, amidst your military duties and the cares which devolve on you in the eminent position you so justly occupy, and the pressing functions, moreover, of your political life. After reading the letter of your Eminence, in which you acknowledge the book which I dedicated to you, I was roused to write this also; for you request me to attend to the statement, which my brother and fellow-bishop Alypius is commissioned to make to me, about the discussion which is being raised by the heretics over sundry passages of my book. Not only have I received this information from the narrative of my said brother, but I have also read the extracts which he produced, and which you had yourself forwarded to Rome, after his departure from Ravenna. On discovering the boastful language of our adversaries, as I could easily do in these extracts, I determined, with the help of the Lord, to reply to their taunts with all the truthfulness and scriptural authority that I could command.

Chapter 2 [II.]—In This and the Four Next Chapters He Adduces the Garbled Extracts He Has to Consider.

The paper which I now answer starts with this title: "Headings out of a book written by Augustin, in reply to which I have culled a few passages out of books." I perceive from this that the person who forwarded these written papers to your Excellency wanted to make his extracts out of the books he does not name, with a view, so far as I can judge, to getting a quicker answer, in order that he might not delay your urgency. Now, after considering what books they were which he meant, I suppose that it must have been those which Julianus mentioned in the Epistle he sent to Rome, a copy of which found its way to me at the same time. For he there says: "They go so far as to allege that marriage, now in dispute, was not instituted by God, —a declaration which may be read in a work of Augustin's, to which I have lately replied in a treatise of four books." These are the books, as I believe, from which the extracts were taken. It would, then, have been perhaps the better course if I had set myself deliberately to disprove and refute that entire work of his, which he spread out into four volumes. But I was most unwilling to delay my answer, even as you yourself lost no time in forwarding to me the written statements which I was requested to reply to.

## Chapter 3. —The Same Continued.

The words which he has quoted and endeavored to refute out of my book, which I sent to you, and with which you are very well acquainted, are the following: "They are constantly affirming, in their excessive hatred of us, that we condemn marriage and that divine procedure by which God creates human beings by means of men and women, inasmuch as we maintain that they who are born of such a union contract original sin, and do not deny that, of whatever parents they are born, they are still under the devil's dominion unless they be born again in Christ." Now, in quoting these words of mine, he took care to omit the testimony of the apostle, which I adduced by the weighty significance of which he felt himself too hard pressed. For, after saying that men at their birth contract original sin, I at once introduced the apostle's words: "By one man sin entered into the world, and death by sin; and so death passed upon all men, for in him all men sinned." Well, as I have already mentioned, he omitted this passage of the apostle, and then closed up the other remarks of mine which have been now quoted. For he knew too well how acceptable to the hearts and consciences of all faithful Catholics are these words of the apostle, which I had adopted, but which he omitted, — words which are so direct and so clear, that these new-fangled heretics use every effort in their dark and tortuous glosses to obscure and deprave their force.

## Chapter 4. —The Same Continued.

But he has added other words of mine, where I have said: "Nor do they reflect that the good of marriage is no more impeachable because of the original evil which is derived therefrom, than the evil of adultery and fornication can be excused because of the natural good which is born of them. For as sin is the work of the devil, whether derived from this source or from that; so is man, whether born of this or that, the work of God." Here, too, he has left out some words, in which he was afraid of catholic ears. For to come to the words here quoted, it had previously been said by us: "Because, then, we affirm this doctrine, which is contained in the oldest and unvarying rule of the catholic faith, these propounders of novel and perverse dogmas, who deny that there is in infants any sin to be washed away in the laver of regeneration, in their unbelief or ignorance calumniate us as if we condemned marriage, and as if we asserted to be the devil's work what is God's own work, to wit, the human being which is born of marriage." All this passage he has passed over, and merely quoted the words which follow it, as given above. Now, in the omitted words he was afraid of the clause which suits all hearts in the catholic Church and appeals to the very faith which has been firmly established and transmitted from ancient times with unfaltering voice and excites their hostility most strongly against us. The clause is this: "They deny that there is in infants any sin to be washed away in the laver of regeneration." For all persons run to church with their infants for no other reason in the world than that the original sin which is contracted in them by their first and natural birth may be cleansed by the regeneration of their second birth.

## Chapter 5. —The Same Continued.

He then returns to our words, which were quoted before: "We maintain that they who are born of such a union contract original sin; and we do not deny that, of whatever parents they are born, they are still under the devil's dominion unless they be born again in Christ." Why he should again refer to these words of ours I cannot tell; he had already cited them a little before. He then proceeds to quote what we said of Christ: "Who willed not to be born from the same union of the two sexes." But here again he quietly ignored the words which I placed just before these words; my entire sentence being this: "That by His grace they may be removed from the power of darkness, and translated into the kingdom of Him who willed not to be born from the same union of the two sexes." Observe, I pray you, what my words were which he shunned, in the temper of one who is thoroughly opposed to that grace of God which comes through our "Lord Jesus Christ." He knows well enough that it is the height of improbity and impiety to exclude infants from their interest in the apostle's words, where he said of God the Father: "Who hath delivered us from the power of darkness, and hath translated us into the kingdom of His dear son." This, no doubt, is the reason why he preferred to omit rather than quote these words.

## Chapter 6. —The Same Continued.

He has next adduced that passage of ours, wherein we said: "For there would have been none of this shame-producing concupiscence, which is impudently praised by impudent men, if man had not previously sinned; while as to marriage, it would still have existed, even if no man had sinned: for the procreation of children would have been effected without this disease." Up to this point he cited my words; but he shrank from adding what comes next— "in the body of that chaste life, although without it this cannot be done in 'the body of this death.'" He would not complete my sentence, but mutilated it somewhat, because he dreaded the apostle's exclamation, of which my words gave him a reminder: "O wretched man that I am! who shall deliver me from the body of this death? The grace of God, through Jesus Christ our Lord." For the body of this death existed not in paradise before sin; therefore did we say, "In the body of that chaste life," which was the life of paradise, "the procreation of children could have been affected without the disease, without which now in the body of this death it cannot be done." The apostle, however, before arriving at that mention of man's misery and God's grace which we have just quoted, had first said: "I see another law in my members warring against the law of my mind, and bringing me into captivity to the law of sin which is in my members." Then it is that he exclaimed, "O wretched man that I am! who shall deliver me from the body of this death? The grace of God, through Jesus Christ our Lord." In the body of this death, therefore, such as it was in paradise before sin, there certainly was not "another law in our members warring against the law of our mind"— which now, even when we are unwilling, and withhold consent, and use not our members to fulfil that which it desires, still dwells in these members, and harasses our resisting and repugnant mind. And this conflict in itself, although not involving condemnation, because it does not consummate sin, is nevertheless "wretched," inasmuch as it has no peace. I think, then, that I have shown you clearly enough that this man had a special object as well as method in quoting my words: he adduced them for refutation in such manner as in some instances to interrupt the context of my sentences by removing what stood between them, and in other instances to curtail them by withdrawing their concluding words; and his reason for doing all this I think I have sufficiently explained.

Chapter 7 [III.]—Augustin Adduces a Passage Selected from the Preface of Julianus. (See "The Unfinished Work," i. 73.)

Let us now look at those words of ours which he adduced just as it suited him, and to which he would oppose his own. For they are followed by his words; moreover, as the person insinuated who sent you the paper of extracts, he copied something out of a preface, which was no doubt the preface of the books from which he selected a few passages. The paragraph thus copied stands as follows: "The teachers of our day, most holy brother, who are the instigators of the disgraceful faction which is now overheated with its zeal, are determined on compassing the injury and discredit of the men with whose sacred fervor they are set on fire, by nothing less than the ruin of the whole Church; little thinking how much honor they have conferred on those whose renown they have shown to be only capable of being destroyed along with the catholic religion. For, if one should say, either that there is free will in man, or that God is the Creator of those that are born, he is at once set down as a Cœlestian and a Pelagian. To avoid being called heretics, they turn Manicheans; and so, whilst shirking a pretended infamy, they incur a real reproach; just like the animals, which in hunting they surround with dyed feathers, in order to scare and drive them into their nets; the poor brutes are not gifted with reason, and so they are thrust all together by a vain panic into a real destruction."

Chapter 8. —Augustin Refutes the Passage Adduced Above.

Well, now, whoever you are that have said all this, what you say is by no means true; by no means, I repeat; you are much deceived, or you aim at deceiving others. We do not deny free will; but, even as the Truth declares, "if the Son shall make you free, then shall ye be free indeed." It is yourselves who invidiously deny this Liberator, since you ascribe a vain liberty to yourselves in your captivity. Captives you are; for "of whom a man is overcome," as the Scripture says, "of the same is he brought in bondage;" and no one except by the grace of the great Liberator is loosed from the chain of this bondage, from which no man living is free. For "by one man sin entered into the world, and death by sin; and so death passed upon all men, for in him all have sinned." Thus, then, God is the Creator of those that are born in such wise that all pass from the one into condemnation, who have not the One Liberator by regeneration. For He is described as "the Potter, forming out of the same lump one vessel unto honor in His mercy, and another unto dishonor in judgment." And so runs the Church's canticle "mercy and judgment." You are therefore only misleading yourself and others when you say, "If one should affirm, either that there is free will in man, or that God is the Creator of those that are born, he is at once set down as a

Cœlestian and a Pelagian;" for the catholic faith says these things. If, however, any one says that there is a free will in man for worshipping God aright, without His assistance; and whosoever says that God is the Creator of those that are born in such wise as to deny that infants have any need of one to redeem them from the power of the devil: that is the man who is set down as a disciple of Cœlestius and Pelagius. Therefore that men have within them a free will, and that God is the Creator of those that are born, are propositions which we both allow. You are not Cœlestians and Pelagians for merely saying this. But what you do really say is this, that any man whatever has freedom enough of will for doing good without God's help, and that infants undergo no such change as being "delivered from the power of darkness and translated into the kingdom of God;" and because you say so, you are Cœlestians and Pelagians. Why, then, do you hide under the covering of a common dogma for deceit, concealing your own especial delinquency which has gained for you a party-name; and why, to terrify the ignorant with a shocking term, do you say of us, "To avoid being called heretics, they turn Manicheans?"

Chapter 9. —The Catholics Maintain the Doctrine of Original Sin, and Thus are Far from Being Manicheans.

Listen, then, for a little while, and observe what is involved in this question. Catholics say that human nature was created good by the good God as Creator; but that, having been corrupted by sin, it needs the physician Christ. The Manicheans affirm, that human nature was not created by God good, and corrupted by sin; but that man

61

was formed by the prince of eternal darkness of a mixture of two natures which had ever existed—one good and the other evil. The Pelagians and Cœlestians say that human nature was created good by the good God; but that it is still so sound and healthy in infants at their birth, that they have no need at that age of Christ's medicine. Recognize, then, your name in your dogma; and cease from intruding upon the Catholics, who refute you, a name and a dogma which belong to others. For truth rejects both parties—the Manicheans and yourselves. To the Manicheans it says: "Have ye not read that He which made man at the beginning, made them male and female; and said, For this cause shall a man leave father and mother, and shall cleave to his wife; and they twain shall be one flesh? Wherefore they are no more twain, but one flesh. What, therefore, God hath joined together, let not man put asunder." Now Christ shows, in this passage, that God is both the Creator of man, and the uniter in marriage of husband and wife; whereas the Manicheans deny both these propositions. To you, however, He says: "The Son of man is come to seek and to save that which is lost." But you, admirable Christians as you are, answer Christ: "If you came to seek and to save that which was lost, then you did not come for infants; for they were not lost, but are born in a state of salvation: go to older men; we give you a rule from your own words: 'They that be whole need not a physician, but they that are sick.'" Now, as it happens, the Manichean, who says that man has evil mixed in his nature, must wish his good soul at any rate to be saved by Christ; whereas you contend that there is in infants nothing to be sired by Christ, since they are already safe. And thus the Manichean besets human nature with his detestable censure, and you with your cruel praise. For whosoever shall believe your laudation, will never bring their babes to the Savior. Entertaining such impious views as these, of what use is it that you fearlessly face that which is enacted for you in order to induce salutary fear and to treat you as a human being, and not as that poor animal of yours which was surrounded with the colored feathers to be driven into the hunting toils? Need was that you should hold the truth, and, because zeal for it, have no fear; but, as things are, you evade fear in such wise that, if you feared, you would rather run away from the net of the malignant one than run into it. The reason why your catholic mother alarms you is, because she fears for both you and others from you; and if by the help of her sons who possess any authority in the State she acts with a view to make you afraid, she does so, not from cruelty, but from love. You, however, are a very brave man; and you deem it the coward's part to be afraid of men. Well then, fear God; and do not try with such obstinacy to subvert the ancient foundations of the catholic faith. Although I could even wish that spirited temper of yours would entertain some little fear of human authority, at least in the present case. I could wish, I say, that it would rather tremble through cowardice than perish through audacity.

Chapter 10 [IV.]—In What Manner the Adversary's Cavils Must Be Refuted.

Let us now look at the rest of what he has joined together in his selections. But what should be my course of proceeding? Ought I to set forth every passage of his for the purpose of answering it, or, omitting everything which the catholic faith contains, as not in dispute between us, only handle and confute those statements in which he strays away from the beaten path of truth, and endeavors to graft on catholic stems the poisonous shoots of his Pelagian heresy? This is, no doubt, the easier course. But I suppose I must not lose sight of a possible contingency, that anyone, after reading my book, without perusing all that has been alleged by him, may think that I was unwilling to bring forward the passages on which his allegations depend, and by which are shown to be truly deduced the statements which I am controverting as false. I should be glad, therefore, if the reader will without exception kindly observe and consider the two classes of contributions which occur in this little work of ours—that is to say, all that he has alleged, and the answers which on my side I give him.

Chapter 11. —The Devil the Author, Not of Nature, But Only of Sin.

Now, the man who forwarded to your Love the paper in question has introduced the contents thereof with this title: "In opposition to those persons who condemn matrimony, and ascribe its fruits to the devil." This, then, is not in opposition to us, who neither condemn matrimony, which we even commend in its order with a just commendation, nor ascribe its fruits to the devil. For the fruits of matrimony are men which are orderly engendered from it, and not the sins which accompany their birth. Human beings are not under the devil's dominion because they are human beings, in which respect they are the fruits of matrimony; but because they are sinful, in which resides the transmission of their sins. For the devil is the author of sin, not of nature.

Chapter 12. —Eve's Name Means Life, and is a Great Sacrament of the Church.

Now, observe the rest of the passage in which he thinks he finds, to our prejudice, what is consonant with the above-quoted title. "God," says he, "who had framed Adam out of the dust of the ground, formed Eve out of his rib, and said, She shall be called Life, because she is the mother of all who live." Well now, it is not so written. But what matters that to us? For it constantly happens that our memory fails in verbal accuracy, while the sense is still maintained. Nor was it God, but her husband, who gave Eve her name, which should signify Life; for thus it is written: "And Adam called his wife's name Life, because she is the mother of all living." But very likely he might have understood the Scripture as testifying that God gave Eve this name through Adam, as His prophet. For in that she was called Life, and the mother of all living, there lies a great sacrament of the Church, of which it would detain us long to speak, and which is unnecessary to our present undertaking. The very same thing which the apostle says, "This is a great sacrament: but I speak concerning Christ and the Church," was also spoken by Adam when he said, "For this cause shall a man leave his father and his mother, and shall cleave unto his wife; and they twain shall be one flesh." The Lord Jesus, however, in the Gospel mentions God as having said this of Eve; and the reason, no doubt, is, that God declared through the man what the man, in fact, uttered as a prophecy. Now, observe what follows in the paper of extracts: "By that primitive name," says he, "He showed for what labor the woman had been provided; and He said accordingly, 'Be fruitful, and multiply, and replenish the earth.'" Now, who amongst ourselves denies that the woman was provided for the work of child-bearing by the Lord God, the beneficent Creator of all good? See further what he goes on to say: "God, therefore, who created them male and female, furnished them with members suitable for procreation, and ordained that bodies should be produced from bodies; and yet is security for their capacity for effecting the work, executing all that exists with that power which He used in creation." Well, even this we acknowledge to be catholic doctrine, as we also do about the passage which he immediately subjoins: "If, then, offspring comes only through sex, and sex only through the body, and the body through God, who can hesitate to allow that fecundity is rightly attributed to God?"

Chapter 13. —The Pelagian Argument to Show that the Devil Has No Rights in the Fruits of Marriage.

After these true and catholic statements, which are, moreover, really contained in the Holy Scriptures, although they are not adduced by him in a catholic spirit, with the earnestness of a catholic mind, he loses no time in introducing to us the heresy of Pelagius and Cœlestius, for which purpose he wrote, indeed, his previous remarks. Mark carefully the following words: "You now who say, 'We do not deny that they, are still, of whatever parents born, under the devil's power, unless they be born again in Christ,' show us what the devil can recognize as his own in the sexes, because of which he can (to use your phrase) rightly claim as his property the fruit which they produce. Is it the difference of the sexes? But this is inherent in the bodies which God made. Is it their union? But this union is justified in the privilege of the primeval blessing no less than institution. For it is the voice of God that says, 'A man shall leave his father and his mother, and shall cleave to his wife; and they two shall be one flesh.' It is again the voice of God which says, 'Be fruitful, and multiply, and replenish the earth.' Or is it, perchance, their fertility? But this is the very reason why matrimony was instituted."

Chapter 14 [V.]—Concupiscence Alone, in Marriage, is Not of God.

You see the terms of his question to us: what the devil can find in the sexes to call his own, because of which they should be in his power, who are born of parents of whatsoever kind, unless they be born again in Christ; he asks us, moreover, whether it is the difference in the sexes which we ascribe to the devil, or their union, or their very fruitfulness. We answer, then, nothing of these qualities, since the difference of sex belongs to "the vessels" of the parents; while the union of the two pertains to the procreation of children; and their fruitfulness to the blessing pronounced on the marriage institution. But all these things are of God; yet amongst them he was unwilling to name that "lust of the flesh, which is not of the Father, but is of the world;" and "of this world" the devil is said to be "the prince." Now, the devil found no carnal concupiscence in the Lord, because the Lord did not come as a man to men by its means. Accordingly, He says Himself: "The prince of this world comes, and finds nothing in me"—nothing, that is, of sin; neither that which is derived from birth, nor that which is added during life. Among all the natural goods of procreation which he mentioned, he was, I repeat, unwilling to name this particular fact of concupiscence, over which even marriage blushes, which glories in all these before-mentioned goods. For why is the especial work of parents withdrawn and hidden even from the eyes of their children, except that it is impossible for them to be occupied in laudable procreation without shameful lust? Because of this it was that even they were ashamed who first covered their nakedness. These portions of their person were not suggestive of shame before, but deserved to be commended and praised as the work of God. They put on their covering when they felt their shame, and they felt their shame when, after their own disobedience to their Maker, they felt their members disobedient to themselves. Our quoter of extracts likewise felt ashamed of this concupiscence. For he mentioned the difference of the sexes; he mentioned also their union, and he mentioned their fertility; but this last concomitant of lust he blushed to mention. And no wonder if mere talkers are ashamed of that which we see parents themselves, so interested in their function, blush to think of.

Chapter 15. —Man, by Birth, is Placed Under the Dominion of the Devil Through Sin; We Were All One in Adam When He Sinned.

He then proceeds to ask: "Why, then, are they in the devil's power whom God created?" And he finds an answer to his own question apparently from a phrase of mine. "Because of sin," says he, "not because of nature." Then framing his answer about mine, he says: "But as there cannot be offspring without the sexes, so there cannot be sin without the will." Yes, indeed, such is the truth. For even as "by one man sin entered into the world, and death by sin; so also has death passed through to all men, for in him all have sinned." By the evil will of that one man all sinned in him, since all were that one man, from whom, therefore, they individually derived original sin. "For you allege," says he, "that the reason why they are in the devil's power is because they are born of the union of the two sexes." I plainly aver that it is because of transgression that they are in the devil's power, and that their participation, moreover, of this transgression is due to the circumstance that they are born of the said union of the sexes, which cannot even accomplish its own honorable function without the incident of shameful lust. This has also, in fact, been said by Ambrose, of most blessed memory, bishop of the church in Milan, when he gives as the reason why Christ's birth in the flesh was free from all sinful fault, that His conception was not the result of a union of the two sexes; whereas there is not one among human beings conceived in such union who is without sin. These are his precise words: "On that account, and being man, He was tried by every sort of temptation, and in the likeness of man He bore them all; inasmuch, however, as He was born of the Spirit, He abstained from all sin. For every man is a liar, and none is without sin, but God only. It has accordingly," adds he, "been constantly observed, that clearly no one who is born of a man and a woman, that is to say, through the union of their bodies, is free from sin; for whoever is free from sin is free also from conception of this kind." Well now, will you dare, ye disciples of Pelagius and Cœlestius, to call this man a Manichean? as the heretic Jovinian did, when the holy bishop maintained the permanent virginity of the blessed Mary even after child-bearing, in opposition to this man's impiety. If, however, you do not dare to call him a Manichean, why do you call us Manicheans when we defend the catholic faith in the self-same cause and with the self same opinions? But if you will taunt that most faithful man with having entertained Manichean error in this matter, there is no help for it, you must enjoy your taunts as best you may, and so fill up Jovinian's measure more fully; as for ourselves, we can patiently endure along with such a man of God your taunts and jibes. And yet your heresiarch Pelagius commends Ambrose's faith and extreme purity in the knowledge of the Scriptures so greatly, as to declare that not even an enemy could venture to find fault with him. Observe, then, to what length you have gone, and refrain from following any further in the audacious steps of Jovinian. And yet that man, although by his excessive commendation of marriage he put it on a par with holy virginity, never denied the necessity of Christ to save those who are born of marriage even fresh from their mother's womb, and to redeem them from the power of the devil. This, however, you deny; and because we oppose you in defense of those who cannot yet speak for themselves, and in defense of the very foundations of the catholic faith, you taunt us, with being Manicheans. But let us now see what comes next.

Chapter 16 [VI.]—It is Not of Us, But Our Sins, that the Devil is the Author.

He puts to us, then, another question, saying, "Whom, then, do you confess to be the author of infants? The true God?" I answer: "Yes; the true God." He then remarks, "But He did not make evil;" and again asks, "Whether we confess the devil to be the creator of infants?" Then again he answers, "But he did not create human nature." He then closes the subject, as it were, with this inference: "Since union is evil, and the condition of our bodies is degraded, therefore you ascribe our bodies to an evil creator." My answer to this is, I do not ascribe to an evil creator our bodies, but our sins; by reason of which it came to pass that, whereas in our bodies, that is to say, in what God has made, all was honorable and well-pleasing, there yet accrued in the intercourse of male and female what caused shame, so that their union was not such as might have been in the body of that unimpaired life, but such as we see with a blush in the body of this death. "But God," says he, "has divided in sex what He would unite in operation. So that from Him comes the union of bodies, from whom first came the creation of bodies." We have already furnished an answer to this statement, when we said that these bodies are of God. But about the disobedience of the members of these bodies, this comes through the lust of the flesh which "is not of the Father." He goes on to say, that "it is impossible for evil fruits to spring from so many good things, such as bodies, sexes, and their unions; or that human beings should be made by God for the purpose of their being, by lawful right, as you maintain, held in possession by the devil." Now it has been already affirmed, that they are not thus held because they are men, which designation belongs to their nature, of which the devil is not the author; but because they are sinners, which designation is the result of that fault of nature of which the devil is the author.

Chapter 17 [VII.]—The Pelagians are Not

Ashamed to Eulogize Concupiscence, Although They are Ashamed to Mention Its Name.

But among so many names of good things, such as bodies, sexes, unions, he never once mentions the lust or concupiscence of the flesh. He is silent, because he is ashamed; and yet with a strange shamelessness of shame (if the expression may be used), he is not ashamed to praise what he is ashamed to mention. Now just observe how he prefers to point to his object by circumlocution rather than by direct mention of it. "After that the man," says he, "by natural appetite knew his wife." See again, he refused to say, He knew his wife by carnal concupiscence; but he used the phrase, "by natural appetite," by which it is open to us to understand that holy and honorable will which wills the procreation of children, and not that lust, of which even he is so much ashamed, forsooth, that he prefers to use ambiguous language to us, to expressing his mind in unmistakable words. "Now what is the meaning of his phrase— "by natural appetite"? Is not both the wish to be saved and the wish to beget, nourish, and educate children, natural appetite? and is it not likewise of reason, and not of lust? Since, however, we can ascertain his intention, we are pretty sure that he meant by these words to indicate the lust of the organs of generation. Do not the words in question appear to you to be the fig-leaves, under cover of which is hidden nothing else but that which he feels ashamed of? For just as they of old sewed the leaves together as a girdle of concealment, so has this man woven a web of circumlocution to hide his meaning. Let him weave out his statement: "But when the man knew his wife by natural appetite, the divine Scripture says, Eve conceived, and bare a son, and called his name Cain. But what," he adds, "does Adam say? Let us hear: I have obtained a man from God. So that it is evident that he was God's work, and the divine Scripture testifies to his having been received from God." Well, who can entertain a doubt on this point? Who can deny this statement, especially if he be a catholic Christian? A man is God's work; but carnal concupiscence (without which, if sin had not preceded, man would have been begotten by means of the organs of generation, not less obedient than the other members to a quiet and normal will) is not of the Father, but is of the world.

Chapter 18. —The Same Continued.

But now, I pray you, look a little more attentively, and observe how he contrives to find a name wherewith to cover again what he blushes to unfold. "For," says he, "Adam begot him by the power of his members, not by diversity of merits." Now I confess I do not understand what he meant by the latter clause, not by diversity of merits; but when he said, "by the power of his members," I believe he wished to express what he is ashamed to say openly and clearly. He preferred to use the phrase, "by the power of his members," rather than say, "by the lust of the flesh." Plainly—even if the thought did not occur to him—he intimated a something which has an evident application to the subject. For what is more powerful than a man's members, when they are not in due submission to a man's will? Even if they be restrained by temperance or continence, their use and control are not in any man's power. Adam, then, begat his sons by what our author calls "the power of his members," over which, before he begat them, he blushed, after his sin. If, however, he had never sinned, he would not have begotten them by the power, but in the obedience, of his members. For he would himself have had the power to rule them as subjects to his will, if he, too, by the same will had only submitted himself as a subject to a more powerful One.

Chapter 19 [VIII.]—The Pelagians Misunderstand "Seed" In Scripture.

He goes on to say: "After a while the divine Scripture says again, 'Adam knew Eve his wife; and she bare a son, and he called his name Seth: saying, The Lord hath raised me up another seed instead of Abel, whom Cain slew.'" He then adds: "The Divinity is said to have raised up the seed itself; as a proof that the sexual union was His appointment." This person did not understand what the Scripture records; for he supposed that the reason why it is said, The Lord hath raised me up another seed instead of Abel, was none other than that God might be supposed to have excited in him a desire for sexual intercourse, by means whereof seed might be raised for being poured into the woman's womb. He was perfectly unaware that what the Scripture has said is not "Has raised me up seed" in the sense he uses, but only as meaning "Has given me a son." Indeed, Adam did not use the words in question after his sexual intercourse, when he emitted his seed, but after his wife's confinement, in which he received his son by the gift of God. For what gratification is there (except perhaps for lascivious persons, and those who, as the apostle says with prohibition, "possess their vessel in the lust of concupiscence") in the mere shedding of seed as the ultimate pleasure of sexual union, unless it is followed by the true and proper fruit of marriage—conception and birth?

Chapter 20. —Original Sin is Derived from the Faulty Condition of Human Seed.

This, however, I would not say, as implying at all that we must look for some other creator than the supreme and true God, of either human seed or of man himself who comes from the seed; but as meaning, that the seed would have issued from the human being by the quiet and normal obedience of his members to his will's command, if sin had not preceded. The question now before us does not concern the nature of human seed, but its corruption. Now the nature has God for its author; it is from its corruption that original sin is derived. If, indeed, the seed had itself no corruption, what means that passage in the Book of Wisdom, "Not being ignorant that they were a naughty generation, and that their malice was inbred, and that their cogitation would never be changed; for their seed was accursed from the beginning"? Now whatever may be the particular application of these words, they are spoken of mankind. How, then, is the malice of every man inbred, and his seed cursed from the beginning, unless it be in respect of the fact, that "by one man sin entered into the world, and death by sin; and so death passed upon all men, for in him all have sinned"? But where is the man whose "evil cogitation can never be changed," unless because it cannot be affected by himself, but only by divine grace; without the assistance of which, what are human beings, but that which the Apostle Peter says of them, when he describes them as "natural brute beasts made to be taken and destroyed"? Accordingly, the Apostle Paul, in a certain passage, having both conditions in view, —even the wrath of God with which we are born, and the grace whereby we are delivered, —says: "Among whom also we all had our conversation in times past in the lusts of our flesh, fulfilling the desires of the flesh and of the mind; and were by nature the children of wrath, even as others. But God, who is rich in mercy, for His great love wherewith He loved us, even when we were dead in sins, hath quickened us together with Christ; by whose grace we are saved." What, then, is man's "natural malice," and "the seed cursed from the beginning;" and what are "the natural brute beasts made to be taken and destroyed," and what the "by nature children of wrath"? Was this the condition of the nature which was formed in Adam? God forbid! Since his pure nature, however, was corrupted in him, it has run on in this condition by natural descent through all, and still is running; so that there is no deliverance for it from this ruin, except by the grace of God through our Lord Jesus Christ.

Chapter 21 [IX.]—It is the Good God That Gives Fruitfulness, and the Devil That Corrupts the Fruit.

What, therefore, is this man's meaning, in the next passage, wherein he says concerning Noah and his sons, that "they were blessed, even as Adam and Eve were; for God said unto them, 'Be fruitful, and multiply, and have dominion over the earth'"? To these words of the Almighty he added some of his own, saying: "Now that pleasure, which you would have seem diabolical, was resorted to in the case of the above-mentioned married pairs; and it continued to exist, both in the goodness of its

institution and in the blessing attached to it. For there can
be no doubt that the following words were addressed to
Noah and his sons about their bodily connection with
their wives, which had become by this time unalterably
fixed by use: 'Be fruitful, and multiply, and replenish the
earth.'" It is unnecessary for us to employ many words in
repeating our former argument. The point here in question
is the corruption in our nature, whereby its goodness has
been depraved, of which corruption the devil is the
author. That goodness of nature, as it is in itself, the
author of which is God, is not the question we have to
consider. Now God has never withdrawn from corrupted
and depraved nature His own mercy and goodness, so as
to deprive man of fruitfulness, vivacity, and health, as
well as the very substance of his mind and body, his
senses also and reason, as well as food, and nourishment,
and growth. He, moreover, "makes His sun to arise on the
evil and on the good, and sends rain on the just and on the
unjust;" and all that is good in human nature is from the
good God, even in the case of those men who will not be
delivered from evil.

Chapter 22. —Shall We Be Ashamed of What We
Do, or of What God Does?

It is, however, of pleasure that this man spoke in
his passage, because pleasure can be even honorable: of
carnal concupiscence, or lust, which produces shame, he
made no mention. In some subsequent words, however,
he uncovered his susceptibility of shame; and he was
unable to dissemble what nature herself has prescribed so
forcibly. "There is also," says he, "that statement:
'Therefore shall a man leave his father and his mother,

and shall cleave unto his wife; and they twain shall be one flesh.'" Then after these words of God, he goes on to offer some of his own, saying: "That he might express faith in works, the prophet approached very near to a perilling of modesty." What a confession! How clear and extorted from him by the force of truth! The prophet, it would seem, to express faith in works, almost imperiled modesty, when he said, "They twain shall become one flesh;" wishing it to be understood of the sexual union of the male and the female. Let the cause be alleged, why the prophet, in expressing the works of God, should approach so near an imperiling of modesty? Is it then the case that the works of man ought not to produce shame, but must be gloried in at all events, and that the works of God must produce shame? Is it, that in setting forth and expressing the works of God the prophet's love or labor receives no honor, but his modesty is imperiled? What, then, was it possible for God to do, which it would be a shame for His prophet to describe? And, what is a weightier question still, could a man be ashamed of any work which not man, but God, has made in man? whereas workmen in all cases strive, with all the labor and diligence in their power, to avoid shame in the works of their own hands. The truth, however, is, that we are ashamed of that very thing which made those primitive human beings ashamed, when they covered their loins. That is the penalty of sin; that is the plague and mark of sin; that is the temptation and very fuel of sin; that is the law in our members warring against the law of our mind; that is the rebellion against our own selves, proceeding from our very selves, which by a most righteous retribution is rendered us by our disobedient members. It is this which makes us ashamed, and justly ashamed. If it were not so, what could be more ungrateful, more irreligious in us, if in our members we were to suffer confusion of face, not for our own fault or penalty, but because of the works of God?

Chapter 23 [X.]—The Pelagians Affirm that God in the Case of Abraham and Sarah Aroused Concupiscence as a Gift from Heaven.

He has much also to say, though to no purpose, concerning Abraham and Sarah, how they received a son according to the promise; and at last he mentions the word concupiscence. But he does not add the usual phrase, "of the flesh," because this is the very thing which causes the shame. Whereas, because concupiscence there is sometimes a call for boasting, since there is a concupiscence of the spirit against the flesh, and a concupiscence of wisdom. Accordingly, he says: "Now you have certainly defined as naturally evil this concupiscence which is indispensable for fecundity; whence comes it, therefore, that it is aroused in aged men by the gift of Heaven? Make it clear then, if you can, that that belongs to the devil's work, which you see is conferred by God as a gift." He says this, just as if concupiscence of the flesh had been previously wanting in them, and as if God had bestowed it upon them. No doubt it was inherent in this body of death; that fecundity, however, was wanting of which God is the author; and this was actually given whensoever God willed to confer the gift. Be it, however, far from us to affirm, what he thought we meant to say, that Isaac was begotten without the heat of sexual union.

Chapter 24 [XI.]—What Covenant of God the

New-Born Babe Breaks. What Was the Value of
Circumcision.

But let him inform us how it was that his soul
would be cut off from his people if he had not been
circumcised on the eighth day. How could he have so
sinned, how so offended God, as to be punished for the
neglect of others towards him with so severe a sentence,
had there been no original sin in the case? For thus ran the
commandment of God concerning the circumcision of
infants: "The uncircumcised man-child, whose flesh of his
foreskin is not circumcised on the eighth day, his soul
shall be cut off from his people; because he hath broken
my covenant." Let him tell us, if he can, how that child
broke God's covenant, —an innocent babe, so far as he
was personally concerned, of eight days' age; and yet
there is by no means any falsehood uttered here by God or
Holy Scripture. The fact is, the covenant of God which he
then broke was not this which commanded circumcision,
but that which forbade the tree; when "by one man sin
entered into the world, and death by sin; and so death
passed upon all men, for in him all have sinned." And in
his case the expiation of this was signified by the
circumcision of the eighth day, that is, by the sacrament
of the Mediator who was to be incarnate. For it was
through this same faith in Christ, who was to come in the
flesh, and was to die for us, and on the third day (which
coming after the seventh or Sabbath day, was to be the
eighth) to rise again, that even holy men were saved of
old. For "He was delivered for our offences, and raised
again for our justification." Ever since circumcision was
instituted amongst the people of God, which was at that
time the sign of the righteousness of faith, it availed also

to signify the cleansing even in infants of the original and primitive sin, just as baptism in like manner from the time of its institution began to be of avail for the renewal of man. Not that there was no justification by faith before circumcision; for even when he was still in uncircumcision, Abraham was himself justified by faith, being the father of those nations which should also imitate his faith. In former times, however, the sacramental mystery of justification by faith lay concealed in every mode. Still it was the self-same faith in the Mediator which saved the saints of old, both small and great—not the old covenant, "which gendered to bondage;" not the law, which was not so given as to be able to give life; but the grace of God through Jesus Christ our Lord. For as we believe that Christ has come in the flesh, so they believed that He was to come; as, again, we believe that He has died, so they believed that He would die; and as we believe that He has risen from the dead, so they believed that He would rise again; whilst both we and they believe alike, that He will hereafter come to judge the quick and the dead. Let not this man, then, throw any hindrance in the way of its salvation upon human nature, by setting up a bad defense of its merits; because we are all born under sin, and are delivered therefrom by the only One who was born without sin.

Chapter 25 [XII.]—Augustin Not the Deviser of Original Sin.

"This sexual connection of bodies," he says, "together with the ardor, with the pleasure, with the emission of seed, was made by God, and is praiseworthy on its own account, and is therefore to be approved; it, moreover, became sometimes even a great gift to pious men." He distinctly and severally repeated the phrases, "with ardor," "with pleasure," "with emission of seed." He did not, however, venture to say, "with lust." Why is this, if it be not that he is ashamed to name what he does not blush to praise? A gift, indeed, for pious men is the prosperous propagation of children; but not that shame-producing excitement of the members, which our nature would not feel were it in a sound state, although corrupted nature now experiences it. On this account, indeed, it is that he who is born of it requires to be born again, in order that he may be a member of Christ; and that he of whom he is born, even though he be already born again, wants to be freed from that which exists in this body of death because of the law of sin. Now since this is the case, how is it he goes on to say, "You must, therefore, of necessity confess that the original sin which you had devised is done away with"? It was not I who devised the original sin, which the catholic faith holds from ancient times; but you, who deny it, are undoubtedly an innovating heretic. In the judgment of God, all are in the devil's power, born in sin, unless they are regenerated in Christ.

Chapter 26 [XIII.]—The Child in No Sense Formed by Concupiscence.

But as he was speaking of Abraham and Sarah, he goes on to say: "If, indeed, you were to affirm that the natural use was strong in them, and there was no offspring, my answer will be: Whom the Creator promised, the Creator also gave; the child which is born is not the work of cohabitation, but of God. He, indeed, who made the first man of the dust, fashions all men out of seed. As, therefore, the dust of the earth, which was taken as the material, was not the author of man; so likewise, that power of sexual pleasure which forms and commingles the seminal elements does not complete the entire process of man's making, but rather presents to God, out of the treasures of nature, material with which He vouchsafes to make the human being." Now the whole of this statement of his, except where he says, that the seminal elements are formed and commingled by sexual pleasure, would be correctly expressed by him were he only earnest in making it to defend the catholic sense. To us, however, who are fully aware what he strives to make out of it, he speaks indeed correctly in a perverse manner. The exceptional statement to the general truth, which I do not deny belongs to this passage, is untrue for this reason, because the pleasure in question of carnal concupiscence does not form the seminal elements. These are already in the body, and are formed by the same true God who created the body itself. They do not receive their existence from the libidinous pleasure, but are excited and emitted in company with it. Whether, indeed, such pleasure accompanies the commingling of the seminal elements of the two sexes in the womb, is a question which perhaps women may be able to determine from their inmost feelings; but it is improper for us to push an idle curiosity so far. That concupiscence, however, which we have to be ashamed of, and the shame of which has given to our secret members their shameful designation, pudenda, had no existence in the body during its life in paradise before the entrance of sin; but it began to exist "in the body of this death" after sin, the rebellion of the members retaliating man's own disobedience. Without this concupiscence it was quite possible to affect the function of the wedded pair in the procreation of children: just as many a laborious work is accomplished by the compliant operation of our other limbs, without any lascivious heat; for they are simply moved by the direction of the will, not excited by the ardor of concupiscence.

Chapter 27. —The Pelagians Argue that God Sometimes Closes the Womb in Anger, and Opens It When Appeased.

Carefully consider the rest of his remarks: "This likewise," says he, "is confirmed by the apostle's authority. For when the blessed Paul spoke of the resurrection of the dead, he said, "Thou fool, that which thou sows is not quickened." And afterwards, 'But God giveth it a body as it pleases Him, and to every seed its own body.' If, therefore, God," says he, "has assigned to human seed, as to everything else, its own proper body, which no wise or pious man will deny, how will you prove that any person is born guilty? Do, I beg of you, reflect with what a noose this assertion of natural sin is choked. But come," he says, "deal more gently with yourself, I pray you. Believe me, God made even you: it must, however, be confessed, that a serious error has infected you. For what profaner opinion can be broached than that either God did not make man, or else that He made him for the devil; or, at any rate, that the devil framed God's image, that is, man, —which clearly is a statement not more absurd than impious? Is then," says he, "God so poor in resources, so lacking in all sense of propriety, as not to have had aught which He could confer on holy men as their reward, except what the devil, after making them his dupes, might infuse into them for their vitiation? Would you like to know, however, that even in the case of those who are no saints, God can be proved to have bestowed this power of procreation of children? When Abraham, struck with fear among a foreign nation, said that Sarah, his wife, was his sister, it is said that Abimelech, the king of the country, abducted her for a night's enjoyment of her. But God, who had the holy woman's honor in His keeping, appeared to Abimelech in his sleep, and restrained the royal audacity; threatening him with death if he went to the length of violating the wife. Then Abimelech said: 'Wilt thou, O Lord, slay an innocent and righteous nation? Did they not tell me that they were brother and sister? Therefore Abimelech arose early in the morning, and took a thousand pieces of silver, and sheep, and oxen, and menservants, and women-servants, and gave them to Abraham, and sent away his wife untouched. But Abraham prayed unto God for Abimelech; and God healed Abimelech, and his wife, and his maid-servants.'" Now why he narrated all this at so great a length, you may find in these few words which he added: "God," he says, "at the prayer of Abraham, restored their potency of generation, which had been taken away from the wombs of even the meanest servants; because God had closed up every womb in the house of Abimelech. Consider now," says he, "whether that ought to be called a natural evil which sometimes God when angry takes away, and when appeased restores. He," says he, "makes the children both of the pious and of the ungodly, since the circumstance of their being parents appertains to that nature which rejoices in God as its Author, whilst the fact of their impiety belongs to the depravity of their desires, and this comes to every person whatever as the consequence of free will."

Chapter 28 [XIV.]—Augustin's Answer to This Argument. Its Dealing with Scripture.

Now to this lengthy statement of his we must say in answer, that, in the passages which he has quoted from the sacred writings, there is nothing said about that shameful lust, which we say did not exist in the body of our first parents in their blessedness, when they were naked and were not ashamed. The first passage from the apostle was spoken of the seeds of corn, which first die in order to be quickened. For some reason or other, he was unwilling to complete the verse for his quotation. All he adduces from it is: "Thou fool, that which thou sows is not quickened;" but the apostle adds, "except it die." This writer, however, so far as I can judge, wished this passage, which treats only of corn seeds, to be understood of human seed, by such as read it without either understanding the Holy Scriptures or recollecting them. Indeed, he not merely curtailed this particular sentence, by omitting the clause, "except it die," but he omitted the following words, in which the apostle explained of what seeds he was speaking; for the apostle adds: "And that which thou sows, thou sows not that body which shall be, but the bare grain, it may chance of wheat, or of some other grain." This he omitted, and closed up his context with what the apostle then writes: "But God giveth it a body as it hath pleased Him, and to every seed its own body;" just as if the apostle spoke of man in cohabitation when he said, "Thou fool, that which thou sows is not quickened," with a view to our understanding of human seed, that it is quickened by God, not by man in cohabitation begetting children. For he had previously said: "Sexual pleasure does not complete the entire process of man's making, but rather presents to God, out of the treasures of nature, material with which He vouchsafes to make the human being." He then added the quotation, as if the apostle affirmed as follows: Thou fool, that which thou sows is not quickened, —quickened, that is, by thyself; but God forms the human being out of thy seed. As if the apostle had not said the intermediate words, which this writer chose to pass over; and as if the apostle's aim was to speak of human seed thus: "Thou fool, that which thou sows is not quickened; but God giveth to the seed a body such as pleases Him, and to every seed its own body." Indeed, after the apostle's words, he introduces remarks of his own to this effect: "If, therefore, God has assigned to human seed, as to everything else, its own proper body, which no wise or pious man will deny;" quite as if the apostle in the passage in question spoke of human seed.

Chapter 29. —The Same Continued. Augustin Also Asserts that God Forms Man at Birth.

Though I have given special attention to the point, I have failed to discover what assistance he could obtain from this deceitful use of Scripture, except that he wanted to produce the apostle as a witness, and by him to prove, what we also assert, that God forms man of human seed. And since no passage directly occurred to him, he deceitfully manipulated this particular one; fearing no doubt that, if the apostle should chance to seem to have spoken of corn seeds, and not of human, in this passage, we should have suggested to us at once by such procedure of his, how to refute him: not indeed as the pure-minded advocate of a chastened will, but as the impudent proclaimer of a profligate voluptuousness. But from the very seeds, forsooth, which the farmers sow in their fields he can be refuted. For why can we not suppose that God could have granted to man in his happy state in paradise, the same course about his own seed which we see granted to the seeds of corn, in such wise that the former might be sown without any shameful lust, the members of generation simply obeying the inclination of the will; just as the latter is sown without any shameful lust, the hands of the husbandman merely moving in obedience to his will? There being, indeed, this difference, that the desire of begetting children in the parent is a nobler one than that which characterizes the farmer, of filling his barns. Then, again, why might not the almighty Creator, with His incontaminable ubiquity, and his power of creating from human seed just what it pleased Him, have operated in women, with respect to what He even now makes, in the self-same manner as He operates in the ground with corn seeds according to His will, making blessed mothers conceive without lustful passion, and bring forth children without parturient pains, inasmuch as there was not (in that state of happiness, and in the body which was not as yet the body of this death, but rather of that life) in woman when receiving seed anything to produce shame, as there was nothing when giving birth to offspring to cause pain? Whoever refuses to believe this, or is unwilling to have it supposed that, while men before any sin lived in that happy state of paradise, such a condition as that which we have sketched could not have been permitted in God's will and kindness, must be regarded as the lover of shameful pleasure, rather than the encomiast of desirable fecundity.

Chapter 30 [XV.]—The Case of Abimelech and His House Examined.

Then, again, as to the passage which he has adduced from the inspired history concerning Abimelech, and God's choosing to close up every womb in his household that the women should not bear children, and afterwards opening them that they might become fruitful, what is all this to the point? What has it to do with that shameful concupiscence which is now the question in dispute? Did God, then, deprive those women of this feeling, and give it to them again just when He liked? The punishment however, was that they were unable to bear children, and the blessing that they were able to bear them, after the manner of this corruptible flesh. For God would not confer such a blessing upon this body of death, as only that body of life in paradise could have had before sin entered; that is, the process of conceiving without the prurience of lust, and of bearing children without excruciating pain. But why should we not suppose, since, indeed, Scripture says that every womb was closed, that this took place with something of pain, so that the women were unable to bear cohabitation, and that God inflicted this pain in His wrath, and removed it in His mercy? For if lust was to be taken away as an impediment to begetting offspring, it ought to have been taken away from the men, not from the women. For a woman might perform her share in cohabitation by her will, even if the lust ceased by which she is stimulated, provided it were not absent from the man for exciting him; unless, perhaps (as Scripture informs us that even Abimelech himself was healed), he would tell us that virile concupiscence was restored to him. If, however, it were true that he had lost this, what necessity was there that he should be warned by God to hold no connection with Abraham's wife? The truth is, Abimelech is said to have been healed, because his household was cured of the affliction which smote it.

Chapter 31 [XVI.]—Why God Proceeds to Create Human Beings, Who He Knows Will Be Born in Sin.

Let us now look at those three clauses of his, than which three, he says, nothing more profane could possibly be uttered: "Either God did not make man, or else He made him for the devil; or, at any rate, the devil framed God's image, that is, man." Now, the first and the last of these sentences, even he himself must allow, if he be not reckless and perverse, were never uttered by us. The dispute is confined to that which he puts second between the other two. In respect of this, he is so far mistaken as to suppose that we had said that God made man for the devil; as if, in the case of human beings whom God creates of human parents, His care and purpose and provision were, that by means of His workmanship the devil should have as slaves those whom he is unable to make for himself. God forbid that any sort of pious belief, however childish, should ever entertain such a sentiment as this! Of His own goodness God has made man—the first without sin, all others under sin—for the purposes of His own profound thoughts. For just as He knew full well what to do with reference to the malice of the devil himself, and what He does is just and good, however unjust and evil he is, about whom He takes His measures; and just as He was not unwilling to create him because He foresaw that he would be evil; so in regard to the entire human race, though not a man of it is born without the taint of sin, He who is supremely good Himself is always working out good, making some men, as it were, "vessels of mercy," whom grace distinguishes from those who are "vessels of wrath;" whilst He makes others, as it were, "vessels of wrath," that He may make known the riches of His glory towards the vessels of mercy. Let, then, this objector go and contest the point against the apostle, whose words I use; nay, against the very Potter, whom the apostle forbids us answering again, in the well-known words: "Who art thou, O man, that replies against God! Shall the thing formed say to him that formed it, Why hast thou made me thus? Hath not the potter power over the clay, of the same lump to make one vessel unto honor, and another unto dishonor?" Well now, will this man contend that the vessels of wrath are not under the dominion of the devil? or else, because they are under this dominion, are they made by another creator than He who makes the vessels of mercy? Or does He make them of other material, and not out of the self-same lump? Here, then, he may object, and say: "Therefore God makes these vessels for the devil." As if God knew not how to make such a use of even these for the furtherance of His own good and righteous works, as He makes of the very devil himself.

Chapter 32 [XVII.]—God Not the Author of the Evil in Those Whom He Creates.

Then, does God feed the children of perdition, the goats on His left hand, for the devil and nourish and clothe them for the devil "because He makes His sun to rise on the evil and the good, and sends rain upon the just and the unjust"? He creates, then, the evil just in the same way as He feeds and nourishes the evil; because what He bestows on them by creating them appertains to the goodness of nature; and the growth which He gives them by food and nourishment, He bestows on them, of course, as a kindly help, not to their evil character, but to that same good nature which He in His goodness created. For in as far as they are human beings—this is a good of that nature whose author and maker is God; but in as far as they are born with sin and so destined to perdition unless they are born again, they belong to the seed which was cursed from the beginning, by the fault of the primitive disobedience. This fault, however, is turned to good account by the Maker of even the vessels of wrath, that He may make known the riches of His glory on the vessels of mercy: and that no one may attribute to any merits of his own, pertaining as he does to the self-same mass, his deliverance through grace; but "he that glories, let him glory in the Lord."

Chapter 33 [XVIII.]—Though God Makes Us, We Perish Unless He Re-makes Us in Christ.

From this most true and firmly-established principle of the apostolic and catholic faith the writer before us departs in company with the Pelagians. He will not have it that men are born under the dominion of the devil, lest infants be carried to Christ to be delivered from the power of darkness, and to be translated into His kingdom. Thus he becomes the accuser of the Church which is spread over the world; into this Church everywhere infants, when to be baptized, are first exorcised, for no other reason than that the prince of this world may be cast out of them. For by him must they be necessarily possessed, as vessels of wrath, since they are born of Adam, unless they be born again in Christ, and transferred through grace as vessels of mercy into His kingdom. In his attack, however, upon this most firmly-established truth, he would avoid the appearance of an assault upon the entire Church of Christ. Accordingly, he limits his appeal to me alone, and in the tone of reproof and admonition he says: "But God made even you, though it must be confessed that a serious error has infected you." Well now, I thankfully acknowledge that God did make even me; and still I must have perished with the vessels of wrath, if He had only made me of Adam, and had not re-made me in Christ. Possessed, however, as this man is with the heresy of Pelagius, he does not believe this: if, indeed, he persists in so great an error to the very end, then not he, but Catholics, will be able to see the character and extent of the error which has not simply infected, but absolutely destroyed him.

Chapter 34 [XIX.]—The Pelagians Argue that Cohabitation Rightly Used is a Good, and What is Born from It is Good.

I request your attention now to the following words. He says, "That children, however, who are conceived in wedlock are by nature good, we may learn from the apostle's words, when he speaks of men who, leaving the natural use of the woman, burned in their lust, men with men working together that which is disgraceful. Here," says he, "the apostle shows the use of the woman to be both natural and, in its way, laudable; the abuse consisting in the exercise of one's own will in opposition to the decent use of the institution. Deservedly then," says he, "in those who make a right use thereof, concupiscence is commended in its kind and mode; whilst the excess of it, in which abandoned persons indulge, is punished. Indeed, at the very time when God punished the abuse in Sodom with His judgment of fire, He invigorated the generative powers of Abraham and Sarah, which had become impotent through old age. If, therefore," he goes on to say, "you think that fault must be found with the strength of the generative organs, because the Sodomites were steeped in sin thereby, you will have also to censure such created things as bread and wine, since Holy Scripture informs us that they sinned also in the abuse of these gifts. For the Lord, by the mouth of His prophet Ezekiel, says: 'These, moreover, were the sins of thy sister Sodom; in their pride, she and her children overflowed in fulness of bread and abundance of wine; and they helped not the hand of the poor and needy.' Choose, therefore," says he, "which alternative you would rather have: either impute to the work of God the sexual connection of human bodies, or account such created things as bread and wine to be equally evil. But if you should prefer this latter conclusion, you prove yourself to be a Manichean. The truth, however, is this: he who observes moderation in natural concupiscence uses a good thing well; but he who does not observe moderation, abuses a good thing. What means your statement, then," he asks, "when you say that 'the good of marriage is no more impeachable because the original sin which is derived here from, than the evil of adultery and fornication can be excused because of the natural good which is born of them'? In these words," says he, "you conceded what you had denied, and what you had conceded you nullified; and you aim at nothing so much as to be unintelligible. Show me any bodily marriage without sexual connection. Else impose some one name on this operation, and designate the conjugal union as either a good or an evil. You answer, no doubt, that you have already defined marriages to be good. Well then, if marriage is good, —if the human being is the good fruit of marriage; if this fruit, being God's work, cannot be evil, born as it is by good agency out of good, —where is the original evil which has been set aside by so many prior admissions?"

Chapter 35 [XX.]—He Answers the Arguments of Julianus. What is the Natural Use of the Woman? What is the Unnatural Use?

My answer to this challenge is, that not only the children of wedlock, but also those of adultery, are a good work in so far as they are the work of God, by whom they are created: but as concerns original sin, they are all born under condemnation of the first Adam; not only those who are born in adultery, but likewise such as are born in wedlock, unless they be regenerated in the second Adam, which is Christ. As to what the apostle says of the wicked, that "leaving the natural use of the woman, the men burned in their lust one toward another: men with men working that which is unseemly;" he did not speak of the conjugal use, but the "natural use," wishing us to understand how it comes to pass that by means of the members created for the purpose the two sexes can combine for generation. Thus it follows, that even when a man unites with a harlot to use these members, the use is a natural one. It is not, however, commendable, but rather culpable. But about any part of the body which is not meant for generative purposes, should a man use even his own wife in it, it is against nature and flagitious. Indeed, the same apostle had previously said concerning women: "Even their women did change the natural use into that which is against nature;" and then concerning men he added, that they worked that which is unseemly by leaving the natural use of the woman. Therefore, by the phrase in question, "the natural use," it is not meant to praise conjugal connection; but thereby are denoted those flagitious deeds which are more unclean and criminal than even men's use of women, which, even if unlawful, is nevertheless natural.

Chapter 36 [XXI.]—God Made Nature Good: the Savior Restores It When Corrupted.

Now we do not reprehend bread and wine because some men are luxurious and drunkards, any more than we disapprove of gold because of the greedy and avaricious. Wherefore on the same principle we do not censure the honorable connection between husband and wife, because of the shame-causing lust of bodies. For the former would have been quite possible before any antecedent commission of sin, and by it the united pair would not have been made to blush; whereas the latter arose after the perpetration of sin, and they were obliged to hide it, from very shame. Accordingly, in all united pairs ever since, however well and lawfully they have used this evil, there has been a permanent necessity of avoiding the sight of man in any work of this kind, and thus acknowledging what caused inevitable shame, though a good thing would certainly cause no man to be ashamed. In this way we have two distinct facts insensibly introduced to our notice: the good of that laudable union of the sexes for the purpose of generating children; and the evil of that shameful lust, in consequence of which the offspring must be regenerated in order to escape condemnation. The man, therefore, who, though with the lust which causes shame, joins in lawful cohabitation, turns an evil to good account; whereas he who joins in an unlawful cohabitation uses an evil badly; for that is more correctly called evil than good, at which both bad and good alike blush. We do better to believe him who has said, "I know that in me, that is, in my flesh, dwelleth no good thing," rather than him who calls that good, by which he is so conformed that he admits it to be evil; but if he feels no shame, he adds the worse evil of impudence. Rightly then did we declare that "the good of marriage is no more impeachable because of the original sin which is derived therefrom, than the evil of adultery and fornication can be excused, because of the natural good which is born of them:" since the human nature which is born, whether of wedlock or of adultery, is the work of God. Now if this nature were an evil, it ought not to have been born; if it had not evil, it would not have to be regenerated: and (that I may combine the two cases in one and the same predicate) if human nature were an evil thing, it would not have to be saved; if it had not in it any evil, it would not have to be saved. He, therefore, who contends that nature is not good, says that the Maker of the creature is not good; whilst he who will have it, that nature has no evil in it, deprives it in its corrupted condition of a merciful Savior. From this, then, it follows, that in the birth of human beings neither fornication is to be excused because the good which is formed out of it by the good Creator, nor is marriage to be

impeached because of the evil which must be healed in it
by the merciful Savior.

Chapter 37 [XXII.]—If There is No Marriage
Without Cohabitation, So There is No Cohabitation
Without Shame.

"Show me," he says, "any bodily marriage without
sexual connection." I do not show him any bodily
marriage without sexual connection; but then, neither
does he show me any case of sexual connection which is
without shame. In paradise, however, if sin had not
preceded, there would not have been, indeed, generation
without union of the sexes, but this union would certainly
have been without shame; for in the sexual union there
would have been a quiet acquiescence of the members,
not a lust of the flesh productive of shame. Matrimony,
therefore, is a good, in which the human being is born
after orderly conception; the fruit, too, of matrimony is
good, as being the very human being which is thus born;
sin, however, is an evil with which every man is born.
Now it was God who made and still makes man; but "by
one man sin entered into the world, and death by sin; and
so death passed upon all men, for in him all sinned."

Chapter 38 [XXIII.]—Jovinian Used Formerly to
Call Catholics Manicheans; The Arians Also Used to Call
Catholics Sabellians.

"By your new mode of controversy," says he,
"you both profess to be a catholic and patronize
Manichæus, since you designate matrimony both as a
great good and a great evil." Now he is utterly ignorant of

what he says, or pretends to be ignorant. Or else he does not understand what we say, or does not wish it to be understood. But if he does not understand, he is impeded by the pre-occupation of error; or if he does not wish our meaning to be understood, then obstinacy is the fault with which he defends his error. Jovinian, too, who endeavored a few years ago to found a new heresy, used to declare that the Catholics patronized the Manicheans, because in opposition to him they preferred holy virginity to marriage. But this man is sure to reply, that he does not agree with Jovinian in his indifference about marriage and virginity. I do not myself say that this is their opinion; still these new heretics must allow, by the fact of Jovinian's playing off the Manicheans upon the Catholics, that the expedient is not a novel one. We then declare that marriage is a good, not an evil. But just as the Arians charge us with being Sabellians, although we do not say that the Father, and the Son, and the Holy Ghost are one and the same, as the Sabellians hold; but affirm that the Father, and the Son, and the Holy Ghost have one and the same nature, as the Catholics believe: so do the Pelagians cast the Manicheans in our teeth, although we do not declare marriage to be an evil, as the Manicheans pretend, but affirm that evil accrued to the first man and woman, that is to say, to the first married pair, and from them passed on to all men, as the Catholics hold. As, however, the Arians, while avoiding the Sabellians, fall into worse company, because they have had the audacity to divide not the Persons of the Trinity, but the natures; so the Pelagians, in their efforts to escape from the pestilent error of the Manicheans, by taking the opposite extreme, are convicted of entertaining worse sentiments than the Manicheans themselves touching the fruit of matrimony, since they believe that infants stand in no need of Christ as their Physician.

Chapter 39 [XXIV.]—Man Born of Whatever Parentage is Sinful and Capable of Redemption.

He then says: "You conclude that a human being, if born of fornication, is not guilty; and if born in wedlock, is not innocent. Your assertion, therefore, amounts to this, that natural good may possibly subsist from adulterous connections, while original sin is actually derived from marriage." Well now, he here attempts, but in vain before an intelligent reader, to give a wrong turn to words which are correct enough. Far be it from us to say, that a human being, if born in fornication, is not guilty. But we do affirm, that a human being, whether he be born in wedlock or in fornication, is in some respect good, because of the Author of nature, God; we add, however, that he derives some evil because of original sin. Our statement, therefore, "that natural good can subsist even from adulterous parentage, but that original sin is derived even from marriage," does not amount to what he endeavors to make of it, that one born in adultery is not guilty, nor innocent when born in wedlock; but that one who is generated in either condition is guilty, because of original sin; and that the offspring of either state may be freed by regeneration, because of the good of nature.

Chapter 40 [XXV.]—Augustin Declines the Dilemma Offered Him.

"One of these propositions," says he, "is true, the other false." My reply is as brief as the allegation: Both are really true, neither is false. "It is true," he goes on to say, "that the sin of adultery cannot be excused because of the man who is born of it; since the sin which adulterers commit, pertains to corruption of the will; but the offspring which they produce tends to the praise of fecundity. If one were to sow wheat which had been stolen, the crop which springs up is none the worse. Of course," says he, "I blame the thief, but I praise the corn. So I pronounce him innocent who is born of the generous fruitfulness of the seed; even as the apostle puts it: 'God giveth it a body, as it pleases Him; and to every seed its own body;' but, at the same time, I condemn the flagitious man who has committed his adulterous sin in his perverse use of the divine appointment."

Chapter 41 [XXVI.]—The Pelagians Argue that Original Sin Cannot Come Through Marriage If Marriage is Good.

After this he proceeds with the following words: "Certainly if evil is contracted from marriage, it may be blamed, nay, cannot be excused; and you place under the devil's power its work and fruit, because everything which is the cause of evil is itself without good. The human being, however, who is born of wedlock owes his origin not to the reproaches of wedlock, but to its seminal elements: the cause of these, however, lies in the condition of bodies; and whosoever makes a bad use of these bodies, deals a blow at the good desert thereof, not at their nature. It is therefore clear," argues he, "that the good is not the cause of the evil. If, therefore," he continues, "original evil is derived even from marriage, the cause of the evil is the compact of marriage; and that must needs be evil by which and from which the evil fruit has made its appearance; even as the Lord says in the Gospel: 'A tree is known by its fruits.' How then," he asks, "do you think yourself worthy of attention, when you say that marriage is good, and yet declare that nothing but evil proceeds from it? It is evident, then, that marriages are guilty, since original sin is deduced from them; and they are indefensible, too, unless their fruit be proved innocent. But they are defended, and pronounced good; therefore their fruit is proved to be innocent."

Chapter 42. —The Pelagians Try to Get Rid of Original Sin by Their Praise of God's Works; Marriage, in Its Nature and by Its Institution, is Not the Cause of Sin.

I have an answer ready for all this; but before I give it, I wish the reader carefully to notice, that the result of the opinions of these persons is, that no Savior is necessary for infants, whom they deem to be entirely without any sins to be saved from. This vast perversion of the truth, so hostile to God's great grace, which is given through our Lord Jesus Christ, who "came to seek and to save what was lost," tries to insinuate its way into the hearts of the unintelligent by eulogizing the works of God; that is, by its eulogy of human nature, of human seed, of marriage, of sexual intercourse, of the fruits of matrimony—which are all of them good things. I will not say that he adds the praise of lust; because he too is ashamed even to name it, so that it is something else, and not it, which he seems to praise. By this method of his, not distinguishing between the evils which have accrued to nature and the goodness of nature's very self, he does not, indeed, show it to be sound (because that is untrue), but he does not permit its diseased condition to be healed. And, therefore, that first proposition of ours, to the effect that the good thing, even the human being, which is born of adultery, does not excuse the sin of adulterous connection, he allows to be true; and this point, which occasions no question to arise between us, he even defends and strengthens (as he well may) by his similitude of the thief who sows the seed which he stole, and out of which there arises a really good harvest. Our other proposition, however, that "the good of marriage cannot be blamed for the original sin which is derived from it," he will not admit to be true; if, indeed, he assented to it, he would not be a Pelagian heretic, but a catholic Christian. "Certainly," says he, "if evil arises from marriage, it may be blamed, nay, cannot be excused; and you place its work and fruit under the devil's power, because everything which is the cause of evil is itself without good." And in addition to this, he contrived other arguments to show that good could not possibly be the cause of evil; and from this he drew the inference, that marriage, which is a good, is not the cause of evil; and that consequently from it no man could be born in a sinful state, and having need of a Savior: just as if we said that marriage is the cause of sin, though it is true that the human being which is born in wedlock is not born without sin. Marriage was instituted not for the purpose of sinning, but of producing children. Accordingly, the Lord's blessing on the married state ran thus: "Be fruitful, and multiply, and replenish the earth." The sin, however, which is derived to children from marriage does not belong to marriage, but to the evil which accrues to the human agents, from whose union marriage comes into being. The truth is, both the evil of shameful lust can exist without marriage, and marriage might have been without it. It appertains, however, to the condition of the body (not of that life, but) of this death, that marriage cannot exist without it though it may exist without marriage. Of course that lust of the flesh which causes shame has existence out of the married state, whenever it urges men to the commission of adultery, chambering and uncleanness, so utterly hostile to the purity of marriage; or again, when it does not commit any of these things, because the human agent gives no permission or assent to their commission, but still rises and is set in motion and creates disturbance, and (especially in dreams) effects the likeness of its own veritable work, and reaches the end of its own emotion. Well, now, this is an evil which is not even in the married state actually an evil of marriage; but it has this apparatus all ready in the body of this death, even against its own will, which is indispensable no doubt for the accomplishment of that which it does will. The evil in question, therefore, does not accrue to marriage from its own institution, which was blessed; but entirely from the circumstance that sin entered into the world by one man, and death by sin; and so death passed upon all men, for in him all sinned.

Chapter 43. —The Good Tree in the Gospel that Cannot Bring Forth Evil Fruit, Does Not Mean Marriage.

What, then, does he mean by saying, "A tree is known by its fruits," on the ground of our reading that the Lord spoke thus in the Gospel? Was, then, the Lord speaking of this question in these words, and not rather of men's two wills, the good and the evil, calling one of these the good tree, and the other the corrupt tree, since good works spring out of a good will, and evil ones out of an evil will—the converse being impossible, good works out of an evil will, and evil ones out of a good will? If, however, we were to suppose marriage to be the good tree, according to the Gospel simile which he has mentioned, then, of course, we must on the other hand assume fornication to be the corrupt tree. Wherefore, if a human being is said to be the fruit of marriage, in the sense of the good fruit of a good tree, then undoubtedly a human being could never have been born in fornication. "For a corrupt tree brings not forth good fruit." Once more, if he were to say that not adultery must be supposed to occupy the place of the tree, but rather human nature, of which man is born, then in this way not even marriage can stand for the tree, but only the human nature of which man is born. His simile, therefore, taken from the Gospel avails him nothing in elucidating this question, because marriage is not the cause of the sin which is transmitted in the natural birth, and atoned for in the new birth; but the voluntary transgression of the first man is the cause of original sin. "You repeat," says he, "your allegation, 'Just as sin, from whatever source it is derived to infants, is the work of the devil, so man, howsoever he be born, is the work of God.'" Yes, I said this, and most truly too; and if this man were not a Pelagian, but a catholic, he too would have nothing else to avow in the catholic faith.

Chapter 44 [XXVII.]—The Pelagians Argue that If Sin Comes by Birth, All Married People Deserve Condemnation.

What, then, is his object when he inquires of us, "By what means sin may be found in an infant, through the will, or through marriage, or through its parents"? He speaks, indeed, in such a way as if he had an answer to all these questions, and as if by clearing all of sin together he would have nothing remain in the infant whence sin could be found. I beg your attention to his very words: "Through what," says he, "is sin found in an infant? Through the will? But there has never been one in him? Through marriage? But this appertains to the parents' work, of whom you had previously declared that in this action they had not sinned; though it appears from your subsequent words that you did not make this concession truly. Marriage, therefore," he says, "must be condemned, since it furnished the cause of the evil. Yet marriage only indicates the work of personal agents. The parents, therefore, who by their coming together afforded occasion for the sin, are properly deserving of the condemnation. It does not then admit of doubt," says he, "any longer, if we are to follow your opinion, that married persons are handed over to eternal punishment, it being by their means brought about that the devil has come to exercise dominion over men. And what becomes of what you just before had said, that man was the work of God? Because if through their birth it happens that evil is in men, and through the evil that the devil has power over men, so in fact you declare the devil to be the author of men, from whom comes their origin at birth. If, however, you believe that man is made by God, and that husband and wife are innocent, see how impossible is your standpoint, that original sin is derived from them."

Chapter 45. —Answer to This Argument: The Apostle Says We All Sinned in One.

Now, there is an answer for him to all these questions given by the apostle, who censures neither the infant's will, which is not yet matured in him for sinning, nor marriage, which, as such, has not only its institution, but its blessing also, from God; nor parents, so far as they are parents, who are united together properly and lawfully for the procreation of children; but he says, "By one man sin entered into the world, and death by sin; and so death passed upon all men for in him all have sinned." Now, if these persons would only receive this statement with catholic hearts and ears, they would not have rebellious feelings against the grace and faith of Christ, nor would they vainly endeavor to convert to their own particular and heretical sense these very clear and manifest words of the apostle, when they assert that the purport of the passage is to this effect: that Adam was the first to sin, and that anyone who wished afterwards to commit sin found an example for sinning in him; so that sin, you must know, did not pass from this one upon all men by birth, but by the imitation of this one. Whereas it is certain that if the apostle meant this imitation to be here understood, he would have said that sin had entered into the world and passed upon all men, not by one man, but rather by the devil. For of the devil it is written: "They that are on his side do imitate him." He used the phrase "by one man," from whom the generation of men, of course, had its beginning, in order to show us that original sin had passed upon all men by generation.

Chapter 46. —The Reign of Death, What It Is; The Figure of the Future Adam; How All Men are Justified Through Christ.

But what else is meant even by the apostle's subsequent words? For after he had said the above, he added, "For until the law sin was in the world," as much as to say that not even the law was able to take away sin. "But sin," adds he, "was not imputed when there was no law." It existed then, but was not imputed, for it was not set forth so that it might be imputed. It is on the same principle, indeed, that he says in another passage: "By the law is the knowledge of sin." "Nevertheless," says he, "death reigned from Adam to Moses;" that is, as he had already expressed it, "until the law." Not that there was no sin after Moses, but because even the law, which was given by Moses, was unable to deprive death of its power, which, of course, reigns only by sin. Its reign, too, is such as to plunge mortal man even into that second death which is to endure for evermore. "Death reigned," but over whom? "Even over them that had not sinned after the similitude of Adam's transgression, who is the figure of Him that was to come." Of whom that was to come, if not Christ? And in what sort a figure, except in the way of contrariety? which he elsewhere briefly expresses: "As in Adam all die, even so in Christ shall all be made alive." The one condition was in one, even as the other condition was in the other; this is the figure. But this figure is not conformable in every respect; accordingly the apostle, following up the same idea, added, "But not as the offence, so also is the free gift. For if through the offence of one many be dead; much more the grace of God, and the gift by grace, which is by one man, Jesus Christ, hath abounded unto many." But why "hath it much more abounded," except it be that all who are delivered through Christ suffer temporal death on Adam's account, but have everlasting life in store for the sake of Christ Himself? "And not as it was by one that sinned," says he, "so is the gift: for the judgment was from one to condemnation, but the free gift is from many offences unto justification." "By one" what, but offence? since it is added, "the free gift is from many offences." Let these objectors tell us how it can be "by one offence unto condemnation," unless it be that even the one original sin which has passed over unto all men is sufficient for condemnation? Whereas the free gift delivers from many offences to justification, because it not only cancels the one offence, which is derived from the primal sin, but all others also which are added in every individual man by the motion of his own will. "For if by one man's offence death reigned by one, much more they which receive abundance of grace and righteousness shall reign in life by One, Jesus Christ. Therefore, by the offence of one upon all men to condemnation; so by the righteousness of one upon all men unto justification of life." Let them after this persist in their vain imaginations, and maintain that one man did not hand on sin by propagation, but only set the example of committing it. How is it, then, that by one's offence judgment comes on all men to condemnation, and not rather by each man's own numerous sins, unless it be that even if there were but that one sin, it is sufficient, without the addition of any more, to lead to condemnation, —as, indeed, it does lead all who die in infancy who are born of Adam, without being born again in Christ? Why, then, does he, when he refuses to hear the apostle, ask us for an answer to his question, "By what means may sin be discovered in an infant, —through the will, or through marriage, or through its parents?" Let him listen in silence, and hear by what means sin may be discovered in an infant. "By the offence of one," says the apostle, "upon all men to condemnation." He said, moreover, all to condemnation through Adam, and all to justification through Christ: not, of course, that Christ removes to life all those who die in Adam; but he said "all" and "all," because, as without Adam no one goes to death, so without Christ no man to life. Just as we say of a teacher of letters, when he is alone in a town: This man teaches all their learning; not because all the inhabitants take lessons, but because no man who learns at all is taught by any but him. Indeed, the apostle afterwards designates as many those whom he had previously described as all, meaning the self-same persons by the two different terms. "For," says he, "as by one man's disobedience many were made sinners, so by the obedience of one shall many be made righteous."

Chapter 47. —The Scriptures Repeatedly Teach Us that All Sin in One.

Still let him ply his question: "By what means may sin be discovered in an infant?" He may find an answer in the inspired pages: "By one man sin entered into the world, and death by sin; and so death passed upon all men, for in him all sinned." "Through the offence of one many are dead." "The judgment was from one to condemnation." "By one man's offence death reigned by one." "By the offence of one, Judgment came upon all men to condemnation." "By one man's disobedience many were made sinners." Behold, then, "by what means sins may be discovered in an infant." Let him now believe in original sin; let him permit infants to come to Christ, that they may be saved. [XXVIII.] What means this passage of his: "He sins not who is born; he sins not who begat him; He sins not who created him. Amidst these intrenchments of innocence, therefore, what are the breaches through which you pretend that sin entered?" Why does he search for a hidden chink when he has an open door? "By one man," says the apostle; "through the offence of one," says the apostle; "By one man's disobedience," says the apostle. What does he want more? What does he require plainer? What does he expect to be more impressively repeated?

Chapter 48. —Original Sin Arose from Adam's Depraved Will. Whence the Corrupt Will Sprang.

"If," says he, "sin comes from the will, it is an evil will that causes sin; if it comes from nature, then nature is evil." I at once answer, Sin does come from the will. Perhaps he wants to know, whether original sin also? I answer, most certainly original sin also. Because it, too, was engendered from the will of the first man; so that it both existed in him, and passed on to all. As for what he next proposes, "If it comes from nature, then nature is evil," I request him to answer, if he can, to this effect: As it is manifest that all evil works spring from a corrupt will, like the fruits of a corrupt tree; so let him say whence arose the corrupt will itself—the corrupt tree which yields the corrupt fruits. If from an angel, what was the angel, but the good work of God? If from man, what was even he, but the good work of God? Nay, since the corrupt will arose in the angel from an angel, and in man from man, what were both these, before the evil arising within them, but the good work of God, with a good and laudable nature? Behold, then, evil arises out of good; nor was there any other source, indeed, whence it could arise, but out of good. I call that will bad which no evil has preceded; no evil works, of course, since they only proceed from an evil will, as from a corrupt tree. Nevertheless, that the evil will arose out of good, could not be, because that good was made by the good God, but because it was created out of nothing—not out of God. What, therefore, becomes of his argument, "If nature is the work of God, it will never do for the work of the devil to permeate the work of God"? Did not the work of the devil, I ask, arise in a work of God, when it first arose in that angel who became the devil? Well, then, if evil, which was absolutely nowhere previously, could arise in a work of God, why could not evil, which had by this time found an existence somewhere, pervade the work of God; especially when the apostle uses the very expression in the passage, "And so death passed upon all men"? Can it be that men are not the work of God? Sin, therefore, has passed upon all men—in other words, the devil's work has penetrated the work of God; or putting the same meaning in another shape, The work done by a work of God has pervaded God's work. And this is the reason why God alone has an unchangeable and almighty goodness: even before any evil came into existence He made all things good; and out of all the evils which have arisen in the good things which He has made, He works through all for good.

Chapter 49 [XXIX.]—In Infants Nature is of God, and the Corruption of Nature of the Devil.

"In a single man rightly is the intention blamed and the origin praised; because there must be two things to admit of contraries: in an infant, however, there is but one thing, nature only; because will has no existence in his case. Now this one thing," says he, "is ascribable either to God or to the devil. If nature," he goes on to observe, "is of God, there cannot be original evil in it. If of the devil, there will be nothing on the ground of which man may be vindicated for the work of God. So that he is completely a Manichean who maintains original sin." Let him hear rather what is true in opposition to all this. In a single man the will is to be blamed, and his nature to be praised; because there should be two things for the application of contraries. Still, even in an infant, it is not the case that there is but one thing only, that is, the nature in which man was created by the good God; for he has also that corruption, which has passed upon all men by one, as the apostle wisely says, and not as the folly of Pelagius, or Cœlestius, or any of their disciples would represent the matter. Of these two things, then, which we have said exist in an infant, one is ascribed to God, the other to the devil. From the fact, however, that (owing to one of the two, even the corruption) both are subjected to the power of the devil, there really ensues no incongruity; because this happens not from the power of the devil himself, but of God. In fact, corruption is subjected to corruption, nature to nature, because the two are even in the devil; so that whenever those who are beloved and elect are "delivered from the power of darkness" to which they are justly exposed, it is clear enough how great a gift is bestowed on the justified and good by the good God, who brings good even out of evil.

Chapter 50. —The Rise and Origin of Evil. The Exorcism and Exsufflation of Infants, a Primitive Christian Rite.

As to the passage, which he seemed to himself to indite in a pious vein, as it were, "If nature is of God, there cannot be original sin in it," would not another person seem even to him to give a still more pious turn to it, thus: "If nature is of God, there cannot arise any sin in it?" And yet this is not true. The Manicheans, indeed, meant to assert this, and they endeavored to steep in all sorts of evil the very nature of God itself, and not His creature, made out of nothing. For evil arose in nothing else than what was good—not, however, the supreme and unchangeable good which is God's nature, but that which was made out of nothing by the wisdom of God. This, then, is the reason why man is claimed for a divine work; for he would not be man unless he were made by the operation of God. But evil would not exist in infants, if evil had not been committed by the willfulness of the first man, and original sin derived from a nature thus corrupted. It is not true, then, as he puts it, "He is completely a Manichean who maintains original sin;" but rather, he is completely a Pelagian who does not believe in original sin. For it is not simply from the time when the pestilent opinions of Manichæus began to grow that in the Church of God infants about to be baptized were for the first time exorcised with exsufflation,—which ceremonial was intended to show that they were not removed into the kingdom of Christ without first being delivered from the power of darkness; nor is it in the books of Manichæus that we read how "the Son of man come to seek and to save that which was lost," or how "by one man sin entered into the world," with those other similar passages which we have quoted above; or how God "visits the sins of the fathers upon the children;" or how it is written in the Psalm, "I was shapen in iniquity, and in sin did my mother conceive me;" or again, how "man was made like unto vanity: his days pass away like a shadow;" or again, "behold, Thou hast made my days old, and my existence as nothing before Thee; nay, every man living is altogether vanity;" or how the apostle says, "every creature was made subject to vanity;" or how it is written in the book of Ecclesiastes, "vanity of vanities; all is vanity: what profit hath a man of all his labor which he taketh under the sun?" and in the book of Ecclesiasticus, "a heavy yoke is upon the sons of Adam from the day that they go out of their mother's womb to the day that they return to the mother of all things;" or how again the apostle writes, "in Adam all die;" or how holy Job says, when speaking about his own sins, "for man that is born of a woman is short-lived and full of wrath: as the flower of grass, so does he fall; and he departs like a shadow, nor shall he stay. Hast Thou not taken account even of him, and caused him to enter into judgment in Thy sight? For who shall be pure from uncleanness? Not even one, even if his life should be but of one day upon the earth." Now when he speaks of uncleanness here, the mere perusal of the passage is enough to show that he meant sin to be understood. It is plain from the words, of what he is speaking. The same phrase and sense occur in the prophet Zechariah, in the place where "the filthy garments" are removed from off the high priest, and it is said to him, "I have taken away thy sins." Well now, I rather think that all these passages, and others of like import, which point to the fact that man is born in sin and under the curse, are not to be read among the dark recesses of the Manicheans, but in the sunshine of catholic truth.

Chapter 51. —To Call Those that Teach Original Sin Manicheans is to Accuse Ambrose, Cyprian, and the Whole Church.

What, moreover, shall I say of those commentators on the divine Scriptures who have flourished in the catholic Church? They have never tried to pervert these testimonies to an alien sense, because they were firmly established in our most ancient and solid faith, and were never moved aside by the novelty of error. Were I to wish to collect these together, and to make use of their testimony, the task would both be too long, and I should probably seem to have bestowed less preference than I ought on canonical authorities, from which one must never deviate. I will merely mention the most blessed Ambrose, to whom (as I have already observed) Pelagius accorded so signal a testimony of his integrity in the faith. This Ambrose, however, maintained that there was nothing else in infants, which required the healing grace of Christ, than original sin. But in respect of Cyprian, with his all-glorious crown, will anyone say of him, that he either was, or ever could by any possibility have been, a Manichean, when he suffered before the pestilent heresy had made its appearance in the Roman world? And yet, in his book on the baptism of infants, he so vigorously maintains original sin as to declare, that even before the eighth day, if necessary, the infant ought to be baptized, lest his soul should be lost; and he wished it to be understood, that the infant could the more readily attain to the indulgence of baptism, since it is not so much his own sins, but the sins of another, which are remitted to him. Well, then, let this writer dare to call these Manicheans; let him, moreover, under this scandalous imputation asperse that most ancient tradition of the Church, whereby infants are, as I have said, exorcised with exsufflation, for the purpose of being translated into the kingdom of Christ, after they are delivered from the power of darkness—that is to say, of the devil and his angels. As for ourselves, indeed, we are readier to be associated with these men, and with the Church of Christ, so firmly rooted in this ancient faith, in suffering any amount of curse and contumely, than with the Pelagians, to be covered with the flattery of public praise.

Chapter 52 [XXX.]—Sin Was the Origin of All Shameful Concupiscence.

"Do you," he asks, "repeat your affirmation, 'There would be no concupiscence if man had not first sinned; marriage, however, would have existed, even if no one had sinned'?" I never said, "There would be no concupiscence," because there is a concupiscence of the spirit, which craves wisdom. My words were, "There would be no shameful concupiscence." Let my words be re-perused, even those which he has cited, that it may be clearly seen how dishonestly they are handled by him. However, let him call it by any name he likes. What I said would not have existed unless man had previously sinned, was that which made them ashamed in paradise when they covered their loins, and which everyone will allow would not have been felt, had not the sin of disobedience first occurred. Now he who wishes to understand what they felt, ought to consider what it was they covered. For of the fig leaves they made themselves "aprons," not clothes; and these aprons or kilts are called περιζώματαin Greek. Now all know well enough what it is which these peri-zomata cover, which some Latin writers explain by the word campestria. Who is ignorant of what persons wore this kilt, and what parts of the body such a dress concealed; even the same which the Roman youths used to cover when they practiced naked in the campus, from which circumstance the name campester was given to the apron.

Chapter 53 [XXXI.]—Concupiscence Need Not Have Been Necessary for Fruitfulness.

He says: "Therefore that marriage which might have been without concupiscence, without bodily motion, without necessity for sexual organs—to use your own statement—is pronounced by you to be laudable; whereas such marriages as are now enacted are, according to your decision, the invention of the devil. Those, therefore, whose institution was possible in your dreams, you deliberately assert to be good, while those which Holy Scripture intends, when it says, 'Therefore shall a man leave his father and his mother, and shall cleave unto his wife, and they shall be one flesh,' you pronounce to be diabolical evils, worthy, in short, to be called a pest, not matrimony." It is not to be wondered at, that these Pelagian opponents of mine try to twist my words to any meaning they wish them to bear, when it has been their custom to do the same thing with the Holy Scriptures, and not simply in obscure passages, but where their testimony is clear and plain: a custom, indeed, which is followed by all other heretics. Now who could make such an assertion, as that it was possible for marriages to be "without bodily motion, without necessity for sexual organs"? For God made the sexes; because, as it is written, "He created them male and female." But how could it possibly happen, that they who were to be united together, and by the very union were to beget children, were not to move their bodies, when, of course, there can be no bodily contact of one person with another if bodily motion be not resorted to? The question before us, then, is not about the motion of bodies, without which there could not be sexual intercourse; but about the shameful motion of the organs of generation, which certainly could be absent, and yet the fructifying connection be still not wanting, if the organs of generation were not obedient to lust, but simply to the will, like the other members of the body. Is it not even now the case, in "the body of this death," that a command is given to the foot, the arm, the finger, the lip, or the tongue, and they are instantly set in motion at this intimation of our will? And (to take a still more wonderful case) even the liquid contained in the urinary vessels obeys the command to flow from us at our pleasure, and when we are not pressed with its overflow; while the vessels, also, which contain the liquid, discharge without difficulty, if they are in a healthy state, the office assigned them by our will of propelling, pressing out, and ejecting their contents. With how much greater ease and quietness, then, if the generative organs of our body were compliant, would natural motion ensue, and human conception be affected; except in the instance of those persons who violate natural order, and by a righteous retribution are punished with the intractability of these members and organs! This punishment is felt by the chaste and pure, who, without doubt, would rather beget children by mere natural desire than by voluptuous pruriency; while unchaste persons, who are impelled by this diseased passion, and bestow their love upon harlots as well as wives, are excited by a still heavier mental remorse in consequence of this carnal chastisement.

Chapter 54 [XXXII.]—How Marriage is Now Different Since the Existence of Sin.

God forbid that we should say, what this man pretends we say, "Such marriages as are now enacted are the invention of the devil." Why, they are absolutely the same marriages as God made at the very first. For this blessing of His, which He appointed for the procreation of mankind, He has not taken away even from men under condemnation, any more than He has deprived them of their senses and bodily limbs, which are no doubt His gifts, although they are condemned to die by an already incurred retribution. This, I say, is the marriage whereof it was said (only excepting the great sacrament of Christ and the Church, which the institution prefigured): "For this cause shall a man leave his father and his mother, and shall cleave unto his wife; and they twain shall be one flesh." For this, no doubt, was said before sin; and if no one had sinned, it might have been done without shameful lust. And now, although it is not done without that, in the body of this death, there is that nevertheless which does not cease to be done so that a man may cleave to his wife, and they twain be one flesh. When, therefore, it is alleged that marriage is now one thing, but might have been another had no one sinned, this is not predicated of its nature, but of a certain quality which has undergone a change for the worse. Just as a man is said to be different, though he is actually the same individual, when he has changed his manner of life either for the better or the worse; for as a righteous man he is one thing, and as a sinful man another, though the man himself be really the same individual. In like manner, marriage without shameful lust is one thing, and marriage with shameful lust is another. When, however, a woman is lawfully united to her husband in accordance with the true constitution of wedlock, and fidelity to what is due to the flesh is kept free from the sin of adultery, and so children are lawfully begotten, it is actually the very same marriage which God instituted at first, although by his primeval inducement to sin, the devil inflicted a heavy wound, not, indeed, on marriage itself, but on man and woman by whom marriage is made, by his prevailing on them to disobey God,—a sin which is requited in the course of the divine judgment by the reciprocal disobedience of man's own members. United in this matrimonial state, although they were ashamed of their nakedness, still they were not by any means able altogether to lose the blessedness of marriage which God appointed.

Chapter 55 [XXXIII.]—Lust is a Disease; The Word "Passion" In the Ecclesiastical Sense.

He then passes on from those who are united in marriage to those who are born of it. It is in relation to these that we must encounter the most laborious discussions with the new heretics regarding our subject.

Impelled by some hidden instinct from God, he makes avowals which go far to untie the whole knot. For in his desire to raise greater odium against us, because we had said that infants are born in sin even of lawful wedlock, he makes the following observation: "You assert that they, indeed, who have not been ever born might possibly have been good; those, however, who have peopled the world, and for whom Christ died, you decide to be the work of the devil, born in a disordered state, and guilty from the beginning. Therefore," he continues, "I have shown that you are doing nothing else than denying that God is the Creator of the men who actually exist." I beg to say, that I declare none but God to be the Creator of all men, however true it be that all are born in sin, and must perish unless born again. It was, indeed, the sinful corruption which had been sown in them by the devil's persuasion that became the means of their being born in sin; not the created nature of which men are composed. Shameful lust, however, could not excite our members, except at our own will, if it were not a disease. Nor would even the lawful and honorable cohabiting of husband and wife raise a blush, with avoidance of any eye and desire of secrecy, if there were not a diseased condition about it. Moreover, the apostle would not prohibit the possession of wives in this disease, did not disease exist in it. The phrase in the Greek text, ἐν πάθει ἐπιθυμίας, is by some rendered in Latin, in morbo desiderii vel concupiscentiæ, in the disease of desire or of concupiscence; by others, however, in passione concupiscentiæ, in the passion of concupiscence; or however it is found otherwise in different copies: at any rate, the Latin equivalent passio(passion), especially in the ecclesiastical use, is usually understood as a term of censure.

Chapter 56. —The Pelagians Allow that Christ Died Even for Infants; Julianus Slays Himself with His Own Sword.

But whatever opinion he may entertain about the shame-causing concupiscence of the flesh, I must request your attention to what he has said respecting infants (and it is in their behalf that we labor), as to their being supposed to need a Savior, if they are not to die without salvation. I repeat his words once more: "You assert," says he to me, "that they, indeed, who have not been ever born might possibly have been good; those, however, who have peopled the world, and for whom Christ died, you decide to be the work of the devil, born in a disordered state, and guilty from the very beginning." Would that he only solved the entire controversy as he unties the knot of this question! For will he pretend to say that he merely spoke of adults in this passage? Why, the subject in hand is about infants, about human beings at their birth; and it is about these that he raises odium against us, because they are defined by us as guilty from the very first, because we declare them to be guilty, since Christ died for them. And why did Christ die for them if they are not guilty? It is entirely from them, yes, from them, we shall find the reason, wherefore he thought odium should be raised against me. He asks: "How are infants guilty, for whom Christ died?" We answer: Nay, how are infants not guilty, since Christ died for them? This dispute wants a judge to determine it. Let Christ be the Judge, and let Him tell us what is the object which has profited by His death? "This is my blood," He says, "which shall be shed for many for the remission of sins." Let the apostle, too, be

His assessor in the judgment; since even in the apostle it is Christ Himself that speaks. Speaking of God the Father, he exclaims: "He who spared not His own Son, but delivered Him up for us all!" I suppose that he describes Christ as so delivered up for us all, that infants in this matter are not separated from ourselves. But what need is there to dwell on this point, out of which even he no longer raises a contest? For the truth is, he not only confesses that Christ died even for infants, but he also reproves us out of this admission, because we say that these same infants are guilty for whom Christ died. Now, then, let the apostle, who says that Christ was delivered up for us all, also tell us why Christ was delivered up for us. "He was delivered," says he, "for our offences, and rose again for our justification." If, therefore, as even this man both confesses and professes, both admits and objects, infants, too, are included amongst those for whom Christ was delivered up; and if it was for our sins that Christ was delivered up, even infants, of course, must have original sins, for whom Christ was delivered up; He must have something in them to heal, who (as Himself affirms) is not needed as a Physician by the whole, but by the sick; He must have a reason for saving them, seeing that He came into the world, as the Apostle Paul says, "to save sinners;" He must have something in them to remit, who testifies that He shed His blood "for the remission of sins;" He must have good reason for seeking them out, who "came," as He says, "to seek and to save that which was lost;" the Son of man must find in them something to destroy, who came for the express purpose, as the Apostle John says, "that He might destroy the works of the devil." Now to this salvation of infants He must be an enemy, who asserts their innocence, in such a way as to deny them the medicine which is required by the hurt and wounded.

Chapter 57 [XXXIV.]—The Great Sin of the First Man.

Now observe what follows, as he goes on to say: "If, before sin, God created a source from which men should be born, but the devil a source from which parents were disturbed, then beyond a doubt holiness must be ascribed to those that are born, and guilt to those that produce. Since, however, this would be a most manifest condemnation of marriage; remove, I pray you, this view from the midst of the churches, and really believe that all things were made by Jesus Christ, and that without Him nothing was made." He so speaks here, as if he would make us say, that there is a something in man's substance which was created by the devil. The devil persuaded evil as a sin; he did not create it as a nature. No doubt he persuaded nature for man is nature; and therefore by his persuasion he corrupted it. He who wounds a limb does not, of course, create it, but he injures it. Those wounds, indeed, which are inflicted on the body produce lameness in a limb, or difficulty of motion; but they do not affect the virtue whereby a man becomes righteous: that wound, however, which has the name of sin, wounds the very life, which was being righteously lived. This wound was at that fatal moment of the fall inflicted by the devil to a vastly wider and deeper extent than are the sins which are known amongst men. Whence it came to pass, that our nature having then and there been deteriorated by that great sin of the first man, not only was made a sinner, but also generates sinners; and yet the very weakness, under which the virtue of a holy life has drooped and died, is not really nature, but corruption; precisely as a bad state of health is not a bodily substance or nature, but disorder; very often, indeed, if not always, the ailing character of parents is in a certain way implanted, and reappears in the bodies of their children.

Chapter 58. —Adam's Sin is Derived from Him to Every One Who is Born Even of Regenerate Parents; The Example of the Olive Tree and the Wild Olive.

But this sin, which changed man for the worse in paradise, because it is far greater than we can form any judgment of, is contracted by everyone at his birth, and is remitted only in the regenerate; and this derangement is such as to be derived even from parents who have been regenerated, and in whom the sin is remitted and covered, to the condemnation of the children born of them, unless these, who were bound by their first and carnal birth, are absolved by their second and spiritual birth. Of this wonderful fact the Creator has produced a wonderful example in the cases of the olive and the wild olive trees, in which, from the seed not only of the wild olive, but even of the good olive, nothing but a wild olive springs. Wherefore, although even in persons whose natural birth is followed by regeneration through grace, there exists this carnal concupiscence which contends against the law of the mind, yet, seeing that it is remitted in the remission of sins, it is no longer accounted to them as sin, nor is it in any degree hurtful, unless consent is yielded to its motions for unlawful deeds. Their offspring, however, being begotten not of spiritual concupiscence, but of carnal, like a wild olive of our race from the good olive, derives guilt from them by natural birth to such a degree that it cannot be liberated from that pest except by being born again. How is it, then, that this man affirms that we ascribe holiness to those who are born, and guilt to their parents? when the truth rather shows that even if there has been holiness in the parents, original sin is inherent in their children, which is abolished in them only if they are born again.

Chapter 59 [XXXV.]—The Pelagians Can Hardly Venture to Place Concupiscence in Paradise Before the Commission of Sin.

This being the case, let him think what he pleases about this concupiscence of the flesh and about the lust which lords it over the unchaste, has to be mastered by the chaste, and yet is to be blushed at both by the chaste and the unchaste; for I see plainly he is much pleased with it. Let him not hesitate to praise what he is ashamed to name; let him call it (as he has in fact called it) the vigor of the members, and let him not be afraid of the honor of chaste ears; let him designate it the power of the members, and let him not care about the impudence. Let him say, if his blushes permit him, that if no one had sinned, this vigor must have flourished like a flower in paradise; nor would there have been any need to cover that which would have been so moved that no one should have felt ashamed; rather, with a wife provided, it would have been ever exercised and never repressed, lest so great a pleasure should ever be denied to so vast a happiness. Far be it from being thought that such blessedness could in such a spot fail to have what it wished, or ever experience in mind or body what it disliked. And so, should the motion of lust precede men's will, then the will would immediately follow it. The wife, who ought certainly never to be absent in this happy state of things, would be urged on by it, whether about to conceive or already pregnant; and, either a child would be begotten, or a natural and laudable pleasure would be gratified, —for perish all seed rather than disappoint the appetite of so good a concupiscence. Only be sure that the united pair do not apply themselves to that use of each other which is contrary to nature, then (with so modest a reservation) let them use, as often as they would have delight, their organs of generation, created for the purpose. But what if this very use, which is contrary to nature, should peradventure give them delight; what if the aforesaid laudable lust should hanker even after such delight; I wonder whether they should pursue it because it was sweet, or loathe it because it was base? If they should pursue it to gratification, what becomes of all thought about honor? If they should loathe it, where is the peaceful composure of so good a happiness? But at this point perchance his blushes will awake, and he will say that so great is the tranquility of this happy state, and so entire the orderliness which may have existed in this state of things, that carnal concupiscence never preceded these persons' will: only whenever they themselves wished, would it then arise; and only then would they entertain the wish, when there was need for begetting children; and the result would be, that no seed would ever be emitted to no purpose, nor would any embrace ever ensue which would not be followed by conception and birth; the flesh would obey the will, and concupiscence would vie with it in subservience. Well, if he says all this of the imagined happy state, he must at least be pretty sure that what he describes does not now exist among men. And even if he will not concede that lust is a corrupt condition, let him at least allow that through the disobedience of the man and woman in the happy state the very concupiscence of their flesh was corrupted, so that what would once be excited obediently and orderly is now moved disobediently and inordinately, and that to such a degree that it is not obedient to the will of even chaste-minded husbands and wives, so that it is excited when it is not wanted; and whenever it is necessary, it never, indeed, follows their will, but sometimes too hurriedly, at other times too tardily, exerts its own movements. Such, then, is the rebellion of this concupiscence which the primitive pair received for their own disobedience, and transfused by natural descent to us. It certainly was not at their bidding, but in utter disorder, that it was excited, when they covered their members, which at first were worthy to be gloried in, but had then become a ground of shame.

Chapter 60. —Let Not the Pelagians Indulge Themselves in a Cruel Defense of Infants.

As I said, however, let him entertain what views he likes of this lust; let him proclaim it as he pleases, praise it as much as he chooses (and he pleases much, as several of his extracts show), that the Pelagians may gratify themselves, if not with its uses, at all events with its praises, as many of them as fail to enjoy the limitation of continence enjoined in wedlock. Only let him spare the infants, so as not to praise their condition uselessly, and defend them cruelly. Let him not declare them to be safe; let him suffer them to come, not, indeed, to Pelagius for eulogy, but to Christ for salvation. For, that this book may be now brought to a termination, since the dissertation of this man is ended, which was written on the short paper you sent me, I will close with his last words: "Really believe that all things were made by Jesus Christ, and that without Him nothing was made." Let him grant that Jesus is Jesus even to infants; and as he confesses that all things were made by Him, in that He is God the Word, so let him acknowledge that infants, too, are saved by Him in that He is Jesus; let him, I say, do this if he would be a catholic Christian. For thus it is written in the Gospel: "And they shall call His name Jesus; for He shall save His people from their sins"—Jesus, because Jesus is in Latin Salvator, "Savior." He shall, indeed, save His people; and amongst His people surely there are infants. "From their sins" shall He save them; in infants, too, therefore, are there original sins, because which He can be Jesus, that is, Savior, even unto them.

Printed in Great Britain
by Amazon